GET
YOUR
SPIRIT
BACK

GET YOUR SPIRIT BACK

break free of negative
self-talk and step fully
into your calling

Foreword by
Louie Giglio

EARL MCCLELLAN

WATERBROOK

Copyright © 2024 by Earl McClellan
Foreword by Louie Giglio copyright © 2024 by Penguin Random House LLC

Published in the United States by WaterBrook, an imprint of Random House, a division of Penguin Random House LLC.

WATERBROOK and colophon are registered trademarks of Penguin Random House LLC.

Library of Congress Cataloging-in-Publication Data
Names: McClellan, Earl, author.
Title: Get your spirit back: break free of negative self-talk and step fully into your calling / Earl McClellan.
Description: First edition. | Colorado Springs: WaterBrook, [2024] | Includes bibliographical references.
Identifiers: LCCN 2024018202 | ISBN 9780593445648 (hardcover; acid-free paper) | ISBN 9780593445655 (ebook)
Subjects: LCSH: Courage—Religious aspects—Christianity. | Confidence—Religious aspects—Christianity.
Classification: LCC BV4647.C75 M37 2024 | DDC 248.4—dc23/eng/20240605
LC record available at https://lccn.loc.gov/2024018202

Printed in the United States of America on acid-free paper

waterbrookmultnomah.com

1st Printing

First Edition

Book design by Elizabeth A. D. Eno

To the love of my life, Oneka.
To Parker, my firstborn son who makes me proud.
To Grayson, my gift from heaven who inspires me.
To Elle, my beautiful picture of God's grace.

The Lord stirred up the spirit of Zerubbabel son of Shealtiel, governor of Judah, and the spirit of Joshua son of Jozadak, the high priest, and the spirit of the whole remnant of the people. They came and began to work on the house of the Lord Almighty, their God.

—Haggai 1:14

FOREWORD

Words matter. Especially your words.

I had coffee with a friend recently whose world has been unraveling for the past few months. His job was eliminated when his company restructured, which put a massive financial strain on his family. He and his wife had been through a yearlong battle with one of their teenage children who was fighting for mental stability in and out of treatment facilities. All the while, an issue with one of my friend's aging parents had resurfaced from the past, and their relationship had become strained to the point of breaking.

I listened for a long time, but then I spoke to my friend. As I listened to what I was saying, I couldn't believe how much sense I was making. How hopeful it sounded. It was as if Peter's encouragement in 1 Peter 4:11, "If anyone speaks, they should do so as one who speaks the very words of God," was happening right before my ears.

I wasn't telling my friend what I thought. I wasn't encouraging him with my wisdom. I was sharing things that he and I both knew were true about God—things proclaimed in God's Word and verified by His faithfulness over the long haul in our lives. I was gently, yet confidently, preaching hope and truth.

In my core, I believed every word. And as I spoke (hopefully as the Spirit spoke through me), the words were landing in the good soil of his heart. We parted, and as I drove away, two powerful thoughts filled my mind: *Thank You, God, for allowing me to encourage my friend*, and *Why don't I talk to myself like that?*

Maybe you're like this too. I've noticed I'm way better at speaking hope and life and future to others than to myself.

That's why I believe so much in what's to come as you let my friend Earl lead you through this freeing message. As he makes clear in these pages, the voice you hear the most is not that of a friend, a family member, a pastor, or a coach. The voice you hear most in life is *your voice*. The question we have to ask is, What are we saying to ourselves?

To be clear, this book is not about self-help but about self-talk. And the self-talk we are referring to is not simply a mash-up of your ideas, thoughts, and opinions. I encouraged my friend with what God had to say, what God thought, how God saw the situation, and how God was working in and through him. You want to speak those same truths to yourself.

The goal is to get to that place where the voice we hear

the most (our voice) is an echo of the voice we need the most (the voice of our heavenly Father).

I love how vulnerable Earl is in this book. It's one of the many things that make him such an inspiration to me and so many. Some of his journey reminds me of a dark season in my life—a time when I was deep in a pit of depression that brought me to a halt. The walls of desperation and hopelessness closed in around me, and I wondered if I'd ever feel normal again.

By the grace of God and the help of others, I made it back into the light. When I did, I was able to home in on a principle that revolutionized my life. It's this: When I speak, I have to examine my words. I found myself saying what many of us often repeat—*Man, I'm not sure if I'm going to make it through this.* Sounds legit and honest, right? Feeling this way is often both legit and honest. But where did that thought come from? Does it sound like something my God would say? Of course not. There's never been a time in eternity when the Almighty said, "Man, I'm not sure if we're going to make it through this." No! He always tells us we are going "through" whatever situation we face. The circumstance might be dire, but God is going to bring us through.

Today, when the thought that I'm not going to make it tries to take center stage, I don't believe the Enemy's lie. Why? Because every time the Enemy told me I wasn't going to make it, it was a lie. Obviously, I am still here, and so are you. I may have some scars. There may have been loss. But by God's grace, I made it, and that reality informs the way I talk to others and to myself.

Even though you've been through a lot, you've made it to today.

I believe by the time you finish this book, you'll see God in a fresh, new way and speak His blessing, power, and possibility over your life. Get ready to get your spirit back!

—Louie Giglio, pastor of Passion City Church
and author of *Don't Give the Enemy a Seat at Your Table*

CONTENTS

FOREWORD BY LOUIE GIGLIO   ix

INTRODUCTION
MORE IN YOU   1

CHAPTER 1
I DON'T LIKE THIS RIDE   9

CHAPTER 2
UNDER THE OAK   23

CHAPTER 3
THE STRENGTH YOU HAVE   41

CHAPTER 4
THE ESSENTIALS YOU NEED   51

CHAPTER 5
DO IT SCARED   61

CHAPTER 6
A HOLY MISSION   71

CHAPTER 7
NOT ENOUGH IS ALL YOU NEED   85

CHAPTER 8
WORDS OF POWER   99

CONTENTS

CHAPTER 9
THE SWITCH AND THE CHASE   113

CHAPTER 10
FINISH WELL   135

ACKNOWLEDGMENTS   153
NOTES   155

MORE IN YOU

Do you ever sense you were put on this earth for more? A feeling that you're destined to touch more lives and make a bigger impact? Are you yearning to make a difference? And yet something keeps you feeling stuck—immobile, frustrated, and confused.

Maybe people think you're full of confidence, void of insecurities, and ready to conquer the world. But there's a voice in your head that says otherwise, and *that* voice is so loud and convincing—it intimidates, bullies, and lies with precision and ease.

I know that voice.

I know what it's like to be in a board meeting, realize the discussion is leaving out an important perspective, and your heart tells you to speak up. But the voice of insecurity tells you to be quiet. And while you're being indecisive, the conversation turns to another topic and you've missed your chance.

I know what it's like to chat with friends and sense God telling you to pray for someone, but the fear of making everyone feel weird keeps you silent. You tuck away the prompt, mumble an apology to God, and shuffle out with another burden on your shoulders.

I know how it feels to long for a better, healthier, more confident future—so much you can taste it. But every time you take a step forward, something pushes you back and says,

> "Sit down."
> "Be quiet."
> "No one will understand."
> "You will look like a fool."
> "You will look greedy."
> "You will look desperate."

All these comments and so many more come to us from within. And they force us back into a box we know we weren't built for.

If any of these scenarios sound familiar, then I'm confident that your finding this book is no mere coincidence. I want you to know I see you. You're kind, resilient, admired, called, and ridiculously loved by God. All that is true. And yet . . .

I see you quitting before you ever start.

I see you disqualifying yourself before you apply.

I see you concerned about what your friends and family will think.

I see you talking yourself out of opportunities before they reach your inbox.

I see you living under the radar.

I see you because I'm just like you.

I played Division I basketball in college. I was a freshman walk-on, which meant I tried out and made the team. The Hall of Fame basketball coach Bill Self was in his first season as a head coach. Going into the Christmas break, we had six wins and six losses. After the break, we lost fifteen straight games. *Fifteen*. It was a *nightmare*. I had never lost that many games in a row in my life. We ended the season 6–21. (As an aside, I worked my way into a starting role my freshman year, partially because so many guys got kicked off the team and partially because I played so hard on defense.)

In my sophomore year, we went 10–17 and ended the season on a multiple-game winning streak, and in my junior year, we started 5–0. We got a Top 25 team vote, which was huge for a small mid-major school.

So we entered a game in Iowa ranked as one of the top fifty teams in the Division I schools (of which there were more than three hundred). I was the point guard (essentially the quarterback in basketball), and we were losing by just a few points when Coach Self called a time-out. He looked me in the eye and told me to take the ball down the court and make a basket for the team. We got back on court,

I dribbled past my man, and I passed the ball to one of my trusted teammates. He took a corner three-point shot and missed. The buzzer sounded, and we lost the game.

In the locker room after the game, one of the assistant coaches sat me down. He put his arm around me and summarized the battle I've faced most of my life: "Earl, Coach told *you* to shoot the ball. He didn't tell you to pass it."

I was happy to give 110 percent to my team. I was happy to hustle hard. Set an example. Be challenged and play my part. I was happy to call plays. I was happy to be a leader, but I was *not* comfortable with people ever thinking I was putting myself above the team. I never wanted to be seen as selfish or arrogant, a ball hog. So when Coach Self told me to shoot the ball, I felt that my teammates might think I was posturing, so I passed the ball instead.

And I lived this way for far too long. I give 110 percent. I work hard. I'm a great teammate. But if a moment comes when I'm supposed to step out and I suspect people will think I'm being prideful, I'll too often pass rather than take a shot. Because no one can think a person who gives 110 percent and shares the ball is full of pride, right? But make no mistake about it—it is pride. And this false humility has held me chained for decades.

When I was about fifteen, my mentor took me to lunch and told me, "Earl, I really want to tell you something, but I'm not sure you want to hear it."

Well, I'm a 3 on the Enneagram. They tell me that makes me an Achiever. I was anxious to know what I needed to know, but I didn't want to hear criticism.

He said, "Earl, you are prideful and rebellious."

Then I punched him in the face. I'm just kidding! I didn't. Those words actually made me want to punch *myself* in the face. It hurt me that bad to know I was letting my mentor down.

Looking back as an adult and a pastor, I would counsel mentors to use different words and to avoid attaching a person's behavior to their identity, especially when they've been made new in Christ. But those words hit me. *Prideful. Rebellious.* I think all these years, in a lot of ways, I've been trying to run as far from those words as possible. And in running from them, I've found myself shrinking back, living with too much fear, not stepping up to my full potential. To others, my life can look great. But I know I have more to give. And you have more in you as well.

I can see you because I see me. I have foolishly imprisoned myself. I confused humility with disobedience, kindness with fear, and confidence with arrogance. For too long I've allowed the grace of God to save me from my old life but not carry me completely into the new life He purposed for me.

For too long I've allowed the grace of God to save me from my old life but not carry me fully into the new life He purposed for me.

So in this safe place between you, me, and the page, let me ask, Who must get out of the way so you can step fully into who God purposed you to be?

My answer is probably the same as yours: Me.

But I'm done. I'm done with the second-guessing. I'm done with the timidity. I'm done with the negativity. I'm done with the hiding. I'm done with the fear, and I'm done with the doubt.

Let's take a journey together. Let's grow together. Let's mature together. Let's be transformed together.

For the sake of full disclosure, I've put my hope in a Jewish Rabbi who walked this earth a couple thousand years ago and who I'm convinced altered the course of human history with His powerful life, death, and resurrection. I'm a Jesus lover to my core. That's why I think I've been so bothered for so long. Bothered with myself and bothered with the current state of things. I'm convinced there is life for all humanity. And these prisons and cages, these mindsets, are holding back too many of us from doing good on earth that Christ initiated through the Cross.

Imagine what our world might be like if those of us convinced of God's goodness became truly free of the mental and emotional traps that hold us back. Imagine a world where good change happened faster and with greater wisdom because no one dimmed the nudges and whispers of the Holy Spirit. Now imagine your own life: How much more free, confident, and energetic would you be if you didn't have to self-edit, self-filter, self-argue at every turn? How would your life unfold if you really believed—in mind, heart, and body—that almighty God loves you and has called you to this amazing life?

Think about all the time you wasted second-guessing. Think about the mental and emotional energy you'd get back if you didn't answer questions from the Enemy of your soul. The whole world got messed up because the first humans decided to entertain a conversation with a serpent (see Genesis 3). And our whole lives have been hindered and at times derailed because we've engaged in conversations that have taken our eyes off God and placed them squarely on ourselves. But feel it for a second. Feel what *could be* by not living in fear, not being weighed down by insecurity, and not being drained by the mental gymnastics your doubts cause you to play. See your life being lived in fullness and freedom. That's what's ahead for you.

Let's be done with the prisons, break the chains holding us back, and find the way to the freedom of becoming who we truly, fully are.

But the kind of freedom we're aiming for is not temporary; it's permanent. Did you know the recidivism rate among state prisoners in the United States is 68 percent within three years of their release?[1] That means those who have been imprisoned keep going back. This is not a book on the issues, problems, and systems that enable and even encourage such an epidemic. But I tell you the rate because I think you and I are up against similar odds. If we want to get out of our personal prisons and stay out, it will require adjustments in relationships, maybe changes to our location, but most important of all, it will require a big shift in our *mind-*

sets! We will have to change the way we think if we want to live free.

We've lost our way, our spark, and we need it back. And we'll have to undergo radical reprogramming. If we're talking about computers, we need to install new processors and not just another software update. If we're talking about a sports team, we need the kind of change that doesn't mean just a new jersey design but rather a new general manager, a new coach, and a new captain. If you're ready to shoot when you're supposed to shoot, pass when you're supposed to pass, lead when you're supposed to lead, serve when you're supposed to serve, and speak up when you're supposed to speak up—if you're done with a hunched-over spirituality and ready to walk out your life with confidence and purpose—then turn the page.

It's time to get your spirit back!

1
I DON'T LIKE THIS RIDE

love physics. There's just something about this science
that really draws me in, and two concepts that truly cap-
ture my imagination are centripetal and centrifugal forces. I
learned about both in Mrs. Tripp's high school physics class
at Providence Country Day School. And after that class, I
started seeing these forces everywhere.

Centripetal force keeps an object moving in a circular
path. As long as the centripetal force continues and everything remains balanced, the object will keep moving in a
circle, like the drum in a washing machine. Or a spinning
yo-yo. And centrifugal force is the pressure you feel when
you're the object moving in a circular pattern, like on that
crazy carnival ride that presses you flat against the wall as

it spins violently and makes you scream like a little kid. You know what I'm talking about: Everyone stands with their backs against the wall of this massive tin-can-of-a-ride with a little chain in front of them. That chain is the only thing that's supposed to keep them from being hurled to their deaths. Yeah, that carnival ride. It has many names, including the Gravitron. (If that doesn't sound like the name of some Decepticon from the world of Transformers, I don't know what does.) Others call it Alien Abduction. Some call it Starship 3000. But whatever the name, this ride from hell that should be outlawed keeps its prisoners pinned against the wall as it spins at warp speed.

When my kids recently asked me to take them on this ride, I politely declined. When they persisted, I offered them funnel cakes because I don't like this ride!

Now all laughs aside, this ride serves as a metaphor for how the children of Israel became stuck in a cycle of their own. Their sin had created a massive amount of force that pushed them in a rhythm they couldn't get out of.

The book of Judges described how this cycle went. The children of Israel forgot about God and instead worshipped idols.[1] This placed them in bondage, slavery, and fear. In their desperation, they remembered God and cried out to Him. God, in His kindness and mercy, heard His children and sent them a judge, a leader. This judge fought to bring them out of their oppressive circumstances and put them in a right relationship with God. They once again worshipped God, and He blessed them. Then the cycle started all over again. They forgot God and found themselves in the chains of bondage, fear, and sin.

Centripetal force. Stuck. Held captive.

And you and I can likely recognize a similar force at work in our lives. When we look at our dating relationships, we might see centripetal force. When we look at our insecurities: centripetal force. When we look at our self-talk: the Gravitron. Stuck against the wall, trying to move, wishing the ride would just stop.

I've had the honor of being a spiritual leader, pastor, and mentor to many different people over the years. And I see the cycles. I see men and women, older and younger, stuck on a ride, desperately wishing to disembark. Not only have I seen these people, but I've been this person.

I like to pray. It's a humbling thing to know that God—the God of the universe, the creator of all things—invites us to speak to Him and to listen to Him. It is overwhelming to think that Jesus Christ, the Son of the living God, made a way for all of us to have an authentic, real, and life-giving relationship with the One who made all things. Wow!

And I love joining corporate prayer—praying out loud with other people. But let me tell you how messed up my head can be in certain situations. One time, about a dozen of us gathered in a circle—assuming postures of humility with heads bowed—praying about the issues our community was dealing with. As we prayed, I felt God nudge me to pray for a specific issue that faced many of us. The words began to form in my mind, and I could feel passion growing in my heart. But before I gave voice to these words, before I allowed the passion in my heart to overflow, I heard this thought: *Earl, you're just trying to get attention. You know these words are just about you. People are going to look at you and be so encouraged, and that influence is going to go right to your head. Be quiet. Don't pray.*

Friends, we're talking about prayer. And I recognize someone could pray and have impure motives—anyone can have impure motives about anything. But the cycle of deception was so strong that even in prayer I allowed myself to cower, to sit silently, all wrapped up in my head and distracted for the rest of the time.

The Gravitron.

Starship 3000.

Centripetal force.

I didn't obey the nudge God put on my heart. Rather, I listened to the same internal bully who told me to pass the ball instead of taking a shot.

In that moment, I made it about me. I let my focus slip from prayer—from God and my friends—to myself. I could not get my arm off the spinning wall. I could not get my mouth to open as the ride in my head spun violently.

I wonder what kind of cycle is running in your mind. What kind of cycle is running in your family, your friends, or your community?

A friend of mine is good marriage material, but he doesn't want to get married because of the negative cycle he's observed in his family. He hasn't seen any marriages last. At least none he wants to emulate. He's spinning in his head. He's spinning and he wants to get off the ride, but he can't. He's stuck. It's not that there aren't great women. It's not that he's not a wonderful guy. It's that he cannot pull himself off the wall.

I bet each one of us can name some areas in our lives

where we cannot pull ourselves off the wall; the centripetal force is too much; the spinning is too violent; the speed is overwhelming. But I want you to know, by the time we are done together, all of us are getting off this ride! We're going to be different people. Better people. More humble. With more fire. More life. It won't be because we're so good; it will be because God is so good. Your grabbing this book is a small way of praying, "God, get me off this ride." And in Jesus's name, we are going to see the cycle be broken.

And to show us how, we'll look at what God does in the life of another person caught up in the spin cycle: Gideon.

First, let's delve into the supporting cast members in Gideon's story, starting with the Israelites.

> The Israelites did evil in the eyes of the LORD, and for seven years he gave them into the hands of the Midianites. Because the power of Midian was so oppressive, the Israelites prepared shelters for themselves in mountain clefts, caves and strongholds. Whenever the Israelites planted their crops, the Midianites, Amalekites and other eastern peoples invaded the country. They camped on the land and ruined the crops all the way to Gaza and did not spare a living thing for Israel, neither sheep nor cattle nor donkeys. They came up with their livestock and their tents like swarms of locusts. It was impossible to

count them or their camels; they invaded the
land to ravage it. (Judges 6:1–5)

The Israelites were just like you and me—normal every-
day people trying to live their lives—but they also had a
beautiful connection with God. The Israelites were God's
chosen people. They were a people through whom the Lord,
by His grace, blessed the rest of the world. And by *bless*, we
mean the ultimate blessing of Jesus Christ. The One who
would forgive us of our sins and give us new life and new
hope and reconcile us to God.

The Israelites were not chosen because of a particular
strength or ability. They were chosen because God wanted
to turn small and insignificant into large and influential.
But pay attention to this: The Israelites needed to get their
now correct so that their *future* would be right. That is to
say, the generation of Israelites in Judges 6 needed to run
their race well so they could pass the baton to the next generation. How they walked with God in their days wasn't
just about them but also about all the generations that
would come after.

> You, too, have a baton and are running your
> race, and someday, you will pass the baton
> on to someone else.

All of us are part of a much bigger story. Not just a
human story. But a God story—one where God is the main

character and all of us play supporting roles in His narrative as He establishes His glory, His goodness, and His kingdom on the earth. So like the Israelites, you also have a role to play by running your race well. And one day, you will pass the baton to someone else, continuing the legacy of this story. Let us not be individuals who drop the baton and thereby negatively affect those who are going to come after us. All of us have had someone go before us, and though it might be hard to imagine, someone someday will be following you. Or perhaps you're well aware of the fact that others are watching your example, and that's why you have a sense of urgency to break the cycle you're in so those coming after you don't have to be stuck on this same ride.

So we have the Israelites. Check.

They are like us. Check.

They are part of a bigger story. Check.

They have a God who loves them. Check.

But they turn from the God who loves them, and they do their own thing. Check.

Judges 6:1 tells us right away that "the Israelites did evil in the eyes of the LORD." That's a bit hard to relate to. Many of us look at our own lives and don't think what we are doing is evil. Especially when we grade ourselves against those we would consider to be the worst of society. But doing evil in the eyes of the Lord in this context really has to do with forgetting not only God but the paths that He laid out for us to live.

When we talk about doing evil in the eyes of the Lord, we mean the things that are atrocious, according to our human standards. But we also mean those things that seem innocuous or benign but in truth are still behaviors that are evil in the eyes of God.

As much as we do good things and as much as we work to be good people, we need to remember that we don't always do right in the eyes of the Lord. I don't say this to produce guilt or shame or condemnation. That's not my aim. That's not my goal. That's not my desire. Nor is it biblical. What is biblical is our understanding that we have all sinned and fallen short of the glory of God.[2] God has a way and a path for us. And this way and path are not just for us to become something great. Our ultimate purpose is to make His name great and establish His love, His grace, His rule, His authority, and His kingdom on earth as it is in heaven. But we fall short. As we learn about the Israelites, we'll find we have more in common with them than we first realized. Try to see yourself in the Israelites—the good, the bad, and the ugly. Because God is about to break the cycle for them.

For seven years, the Lord "gave [Israel] into the hands of the Midianites." The Midianites are the descendants of Midian, son of Abraham.[3] These Midianites show up multiple times in the beginning of the Bible. After fleeing Egypt, Moses lived with the Midianites for forty years. Moses was roaming the Midian hillsides, watching over flocks of sheep, when God revealed Himself in the burning bush. Moses married a woman named Zipporah, and she was a daughter of a Midian priest named Jethro.[4] It was Jethro who advised Moses on how to create a system of leadership that would allow both him and the people to flourish under God.[5] But things didn't always stay good between the children of Israel and the people of Midian. The Midianites and the Moabites convinced the Israelites to worship a false god: Baal Peor.[6]

There's even a pretty intense moment in the book of Numbers when a Midianite princess named Kozbi hooked up with Zimri, and the consequences of that one-night stand were tragic for both of them.[7] The Midianites partnered with the Moabites against the Israelites, and the Moabite king hired a prophet to curse God's chosen people.[8]

Later on, there was a war that the children of Israel waged against the Midianites, and the Israelites absolutely decimated the Midianites.[9] They basically killed all the men, but the Midianites were not completely destroyed. There were enough of them left that their tribe grew and eventually invaded and oppressed the Israelites so much that the Israelites were forced to move into the mountain cliffs, caves, and hideouts. Seems to me that the Midianites enjoyed pressing the Israelites. They thought about how the Israelites had hurt, demolished, and virtually annihilated them years earlier. Now they could exact their revenge. Every time the Israelites planted crops, the Midianites showed up to destroy their crops. They did not spare one living thing in Israel. Not the sheep, not the cattle, not the donkeys. As a matter of fact, the Midianites and these other invaders brought their own livestock and their own homes and tents, and then they descended upon the land of Israel and, as the Bible puts it, "invaded the land to ravage it."[10] The economy was so bad. The oppression was so intense.

The Gravitron was overwhelming. The Israelites cried out to the Lord for help.

Your age and geographical location play a significant role in shaping your perception of empowerment, poverty, and the societal frameworks existing in various nations. These factors will give you your own unique viewpoint on this text in the Bible. I would never want to paint the picture that those who find themselves in a place of oppression and difficulty are there as a result of their own sin. That would be foolish, and I'm deeply empathetic to the nuances and seasons of different people and countries. We are simply looking at this situation in this text of the Bible. And this text is telling us that because of the cycle, because of the sin, because the Israelites had done evil in the eyes of the Lord, the Lord allowed the Midianites to prevail over them so that He could one day bring the Israelites back under His protection. And there's nothing quite like pain and struggle to open our eyes to our desperate need of God.

For seven years, they struggle. For seven years, they are hiding out. For seven years, they don't want to show themselves on social media, they don't want to go to work, they don't want to try out for the team, and they don't want to start a company. For seven years, all their work is destroyed. What they plant does not feed their family; it feeds their enemy. For seven years, they find themselves fighting, scratching, and climbing just to get by. Yes, babies are born, teenagers grow up, and people are still moving about. But life is limited. Joy is not radiating throughout the community. The struggle and pain of these years are taking a hefty emotional and mental toll.

I hate to bring it up, but do you remember 2020? I know during the pandemic some people didn't skip a beat. And some people really flourished in that time. But for the rest of us, 2020 straight-up sucked. We experienced so much compounded tension, so much difficulty racially, politically, and economically. So many businesses didn't make it through that season. So many relationships fractured during that year. From school to work to friendships, everything felt negatively impacted. Don't get me wrong; we made it work. We stood six feet away from our neighbors, all afraid to shake one another's hands. We washed our hands religiously. Our kindergarteners attended classes on Zoom.

That one year felt like seven years' worth of difficulty and pain. Many of us could not travel to see loved ones. We have a church in Guatemala, and our campus pastors were allowed to buy only one or two eggs at the store. They found themselves wandering through the streets, standing in multiple lines, so they could buy enough eggs from different shops. There was even an evening curfew. It was a lockdown.

I think this is what the children of Israel were feeling in Judges 6: locked down. No freedom of movement. *Where am I going next? Can I sleep tonight in peace? What will my kids' world look like in the future? Will life ever be normal again?*

So here we have a people who are struggling to find their way back to life. How is this true for you right now? Has it already been seven years for you? Has it been seventeen years? How many years or months has it been since you've not had freedom of movement in your mind, your words, your money, or your purpose? How long has it been since you harvested what you planted? How long has the centripetal force kept you stuck?

And let's go a half step further. Who are your Midianites? Perhaps your own self-talk? Your family members, your friend circle, or your co-workers? Who or what is taking up so much space in your brain and heart that you moved from the land you are called to occupy to hiding away in cliffs on the mountainside? Identify what Midian looks like in your life. Put a name on the swarm that is occupying the land in your mind.

Give the enemy a name.

You will win this battle. But you will not win this battle with worry.

No, worry is not the way through. You are going to win this battle another way.

> You will win this battle. But you will not win this battle with worry.

"Midian so impoverished the Israelites that they cried out to the Lord for help."[11] Be hopeful, my friends, that just like the Israelites, we can also cry out to the Lord for help. That is, in fact, what we are doing, even as we meet together in the words of this book. We are crying out to the Lord for help.

I don't know if the Israelites cried out in the first year, the second, the fifth, or the seventh. But what I do know is, they cried out to the Lord for help. And anytime we cry out to the Lord for help, He hears us.

I encourage you to take some time, even now. Take some time and ask the Lord for help. It doesn't have to be flashy. It doesn't have to be eloquent. Just like a child speaking to their mom or dad, let your loving Father know you want help. "God opposes the proud but shows favor to the humble."[12] So as we admit our need, we help posture ourselves in a place of humility that opens us up to the very grace we need to find the freedom we seek.

By the grace of God, you're going to get your spirit back! You're going to get your fight back. You're going to get your whole life back. You're going to break the cycle you're in. All of that is going to happen through prayer. We're not aiming for some temporary break. We're after breakthrough.

Since I've played basketball for so long, my knees have taken a bit of a beating. You know how it is when you've spent your entire life dunking on people, flying through the lane, gliding like an eagle, hovering over a ten-foot-tall basket with ease and grace (I'm only slightly exaggerating). Come on, you know what I'm talking about. So I was having some knee pain and went to the doctor. And I had a choice: I could just live with it, or I could get my knee scoped. If I lived with it, I could still function. I could still play with my kids. I could still rebound and play pickup basketball. But popping Advil and beating down my liver for the remaining years of my life was not something I wanted to do. I didn't want to *just live with it.* I wanted to live. I did not want to tolerate it. I wanted to terminate it. So I got my knee scoped.

I took the anesthesia and let the surgeon do a deep work. The deep work cost more. The deep work had more rehab. The deep work required longer rest. The deep work took me out from playing in the short term, but it was designed to keep me playing for the long term.

This book, the motivation behind these words, is to encourage and equip you to allow the Great Surgeon to do the deep work. No longer will we just pop pills to medicate the dizziness of the cycles we find ourselves in. No, we're going after the stuff that is underneath the surface. We're going to the root of the problem. We're going to confront the enemies that stand against us. And we'll discover again—or perhaps for the first time—freedom of movement. And as Philippians 1:6 reminds us, "he who began a good work in you [and in me] will carry it on to completion."

2
UNDER THE OAK

The angel of the LORD came and sat down under
the oak in Ophrah that belonged to Joash the
Abiezrite, where his son Gideon was threshing
wheat in a winepress to keep it from the Midianites.
—JUDGES 6:11

There are moments that mark us, that change our lives forever. Had we not experienced these, we would not be who or where we are today. This is what happened for Gideon.

Picture dusty hills and wide-open plains, something like a mix between West Texas and California. In a town the size of Rhode Island, there was a man hard at work to provide for his family, to better the lives of those around him, despite enemy raiders regularly destroying everything he tried to build. He was an honorable man, not perfect but respected. The type of man you would want your daughter to marry—faithful and steady. He had a gift for leadership that was hidden under fear and self-doubt.

But then one day, while our man Gideon was going about

his work, the angel of the Lord showed up and took a seat under the oak nearby.

It was such a simple moment and yet so spectacular because it changed everything for Gideon.

One of those life-altering moments for me was meeting my wife. It was a cloudy Oklahoma day in January during my freshman year of college. Warm enough for me to wear my sweat suit without a jacket. As I was on my way to basketball practice, I saw a young lady walking toward me with long, black, shiny hair. She wore a fitted jean jacket, and her skin was a rich mocha. She had beautiful almond-shaped eyes. I smiled at her, just enough so she knew I noticed her. She smiled back. That smile removed every cloud above and increased the temperature of the earth by a full forty-five degrees. I don't think I'd ever felt as much life and joy as I did seeing that smile. I got to basketball practice, and as we were doing our warm-ups and stretching, I told one of my boys on the team, "There's a goddess on campus."

Fast-forward a couple of weeks, and Oneka and I found ourselves sitting across from each other in the food court. This was my first chance to have a conversation with this beautiful California queen—and it went well! Oneka's hairstyle made this perfectly shaped slope right above her forehead. It was quite inviting, but I do think using the word *slope* is going to get me in trouble when she reads this. Hey, I'm bald. I haven't had a hairstyle since Michael Jordan started shaving his head. What do I know?

But the moment of our first meeting led to our first conversation, which led to our first date, and later on I asked her to marry me. And my life has never been the same.

Meeting Oneka that day in January was an under-the-oak moment. Under-the-oak moments happen to all of us. Sometimes it's a phone call or a conversation or a photo or a test result that changes the way we see ourselves or the world. Moments mark the stories of our lives.

Here's how authors Chip and Dan Heath talk about it in their book *The Power of Moments:*

> For an individual human being, moments are the thing. Moments are what we remember and what we cherish. Certainly we might celebrate achieving a goal, such as completing a marathon or landing a significant client—but the achievement is embedded in a moment.
>
> Every culture has its prescribed set of big moments: birthdays and weddings and graduations, of course, but also holiday celebrations and funeral rites and political traditions. They seem "natural" to us. But notice that every last one of them was invented, dreamed up by anonymous authors who wanted to give shape to time. This is what we mean by "thinking in moments": to recognize where the prose of life needs punctuation.[1]

Moments are what make us.

We never know when a moment is going to happen. We're just going through life and it hits us. I didn't know that day in January that I was gonna meet my wife. It was just a plain old day. My guess is that it was the same for you the day you met your spouse, received the diagnosis, got that call, had that life-changing conversation.

God in His grace doesn't tell us ahead of time about every single pivotal moment of our lives. I'm not sure we could handle that. I have a sneaking suspicion we would try to take matters into our own hands and accidentally mess up something that was meant to be incredibly special. Maybe I would have overdressed and worn a suit instead of sweats. (I found out later that Oneka was not into athletic guys. Little did she know that God wanted to expand her palate. Ha!) Maybe instead of simply smiling, I would have tried too hard and said something awkward. You know what I mean, right? Think about the nerves that hit you when you know a big moment is coming. God in His kindness allows us to walk through life not knowing precisely when everything is about to change.

We may not know when the moments will come our way, but we can better prepare to *receive* them when they do. We can maximize the moments—because our God is a good and gracious God who is looking to draw us closer to Him and conform us into the image of His Son, Jesus—and walk fully in the purpose that God has designed for us.

KNOW YOUR WORTH

We must recalibrate our worth and our value. If I had not seen myself as worthy of a relationship, then crossing paths with my future wife would have done me no good. I would've already talked myself out of what God was bringing to me before it ever arrived.

We're talking about no longer determining our worth by the standards of our culture. That is to say, your academic accomplishments are not what validate you—a public or private school, a GED or a PhD. They are not your measure of worth. Your worth is not determined by your social media followers, reposts, or likes. It is not determined by your expense report or your child's behavior. Your value is not determined by your position on a team, the size of your waist, or the amount of weight you can bench-press. Additionally, the connections you have with friends, the number of stocks you hold, and the amount of money in your checking account do not determine your value. Your worth is inherent and cannot be measured by these external factors.

This isn't easy to digest, but it is necessary for us to get to a place of rest and confidence. If none of these things determine your worth or value, then what does? What is it that dictates how valuable we are to one another and how valuable we are as individuals? A favorite Bible verse for many is John 3:16: "God so loved the world that he gave his one and only Son, that whoever believes in him shall not perish but have eternal life." And Romans 5:8 reads, "While we were still sinners, Christ died for us." Then, in the very first book of the Bible, Genesis, we see clearly that "God created mankind in his own image, in the image of God he created them; male and female he created them. God blessed them and said to them, 'Be fruitful and increase in number;

fill the earth.'"[2] These are but a few of many verses that establish the worth and value of a human being.

You are loved by God.

Christ gave His life for you.

You are made in the image of God.

You are blessed and have purpose.

These verses, and others like them, are not an announcement that we have arrived and are no longer in need of development, direction, correction, or guidance. Just because we are fully loved does not mean we are fully mature. Look at toddlers. Their parents love them unconditionally, but each child is still on the road to development and maturity. And yes, every child will develop differently and at their own pace, but they are not loved any less. Parents try to help their child reach their full potential. Even developmental delays are not an excuse to avoid seeking growth.

God loves you unconditionally, and His desire is for you to mature and maximize the potential He's put in you. You are surrounded by the love and grace of God found in the death, burial, and resurrection of Jesus Christ. That means your worth and your value do not fluctuate, because God is love and the work of Jesus Christ is finished.

My wife loves to shop for clothes. And she loves a good deal. She'll even notice what some person of influence is wearing, and she has the investigative fortitude to find the knockoff so she can rock that designer look for a discounted price. I am all for that. I'm extremely grateful she has this ability. It has saved me, on many occasions, from feeling the need to give plasma so my wife can wear beautiful clothes. She knows how to find great deals, often discovering pieces that have been marked down three or four times from their original price.

> **If Jesus thought you worthy enough to die for, you have incredible, unperishable worth.**

Some of us feel like discounted shirts. There was a day when we felt we were worth a bunch, but then we sat on the rack or in the warehouse for a certain period of time, and now we think our value has gone down. Maybe we begin to put it out there in our words and body language that we will accept less. But I would like you to consider for a moment how God truly sees you. You don't lose your worth and value because someone spilled something on you or because the seasons changed. No, my friend, that's not how it works with God. That might be how it works in your family or in your friend group. It may even be how it works in your mind. But allow me to insert the truth: If Jesus thought you worthy enough to die for, you have incredible, unperishable worth. Jesus's sacrifice was made willfully, obediently, and joyfully for you. So live into that worth for the glory of God.

COMPARISON

Not all comparison is bad. Healthy comparison pushes us to do amazing and wonderful things we thought were impossible before we watched someone else give it a go. But the comparison that can keep us from recognizing our moments is the kind that pushes us down or leads us to push others down in order to build ourselves up. It's a comparison that leads to jealousy.

If we go all the way back to the original Ten Commandments, we hear God speak through Moses to the children of Israel, and to all of us, "You shall not covet."³ God tells us to stop wishing and wanting their life, their family, their (fill in the blank). It's toxic. That thirst can never be quenched, because that type of envy is rooted in darkness, not in the light of the glorious gospel of Jesus Christ.

One way I've learned to cope with comparison is to pray for those I may compare myself to. I pray big prayers for them. I pray as much hope, life, and strength into them as I can. And as I pray for them, I see God taking my heart and purifying it so I see others the way He wants them to be seen. I have not mastered this, and I would not dare say I have reached Yoda level yet, but I do "press on toward the goal to win the prize for which God has called me."⁴

> I don't want to miss a moment that God has for me because I was too busy comparing myself to something He did not set aside for me.

I'll also take breaks from social media when I find my mind drifting to places I don't want to go. If someone's highlight reel causes me high anxiety, that's not a problem with them—the problem lies within me. And I don't want to miss a moment that God has for me because I was too busy comparing myself to something He did not set aside for me. Keeping comparison in its place allows me to fully enjoy the moments God has for me, and the moments He has for others, because I have matured to a place where someone else's blessing is not my burden.

OFFENSE AND BITTERNESS

In all my years as a pastor, I've never seen anything stop more people from their under-the-oak moments than offense and bitterness. Are you mad or resentful toward anyone right now? Be honest—is there someone who is just an absolute annoyance to you? Is there a person who causes jealousy or disgust to rise in you when you see their photos online, hear their name, or run into them at the gym? When a person has hurt us deeply or bothers us consistently, we have strong reactions.

Say, for instance, your significant other cheated on you, or your parent walked out on your family when you were a kid. The hole they left could affect every area of your life—clouding your decisions, negatively influencing your relationships, and causing you to unintentionally sabotage moments that God has for you.

When people take something from us, they create a debt. Sometimes they know they've done it, and other times they don't. But you are the one left with the deficit. When you carry around a sense of bitterness or offense, you constantly bear the weight of this debt.

My wife and I had student loans for quite some time, and the loan holder kept coming to us each month until every penny, plus interest, was paid. You can keep trying to get those who hurt you to pay back what they took, but they may not have the emotional capacity or the maturity. So what do you do then?

There are two ways to get rid of a debt: Either it's forgiven or it's paid in full. Those are the only options.

I've found that when we expect someone else to pay in full, no payment is big enough, because only we know the size of the emotional or mental debt we've been carrying. Someone might be able to make a little payment toward the debt, but it never fully satisfies. So are we to live in a place of bondage and miss the opportunities that God has set aside for us? Are we to allow the shortcomings of a family member or an ex or a coach to keep us from the future that God has for us? Will we allow what they did to override what God wants to do in our lives?

Please understand I'm not excusing the bad behavior and the hurt and the pain that have been caused intentionally or unintentionally by someone in your life. Forgiveness is not about validating the offensive action. Forgiveness is about freeing yourself from carrying a debt.

Forgiveness is a powerful tool God has put in your hands so no one can keep you captive against your will.

If you want to be free, you will need to forgive. Because every debt, in some way or another, needs to be paid. Many of us are looking to friends and family to make up the deficit. Or we are trying to pay the debt ourselves that someone else imposed on us. As long as our energy is wrapped up in carrying the debt, we won't have the capacity to receive the inheritance God has prepared for us. Forgiveness is key to your future. Forgiveness is a powerful tool God has put in your hands so no one can keep you captive against your will. So don't miss another moment. Don't allow the past to steal from your purpose. Don't allow what someone else did to stand in the way of what God is wanting to do for you and through you. The days of what happened long ago are over! You are a free son or daughter of almighty God.

You, my friend, have the power in your hands—given to you by the grace and power of the cross of Jesus Christ—to release someone from what they did so that you can be free to be who you are called to be.

Just like I had you identify your enemy's name, I'm gonna need you to write down the names of those who disappointed and hurt you, and what they did. Now speak each name out loud and say, "I forgive you."

I'm not saying you'll ever lose the memory—I wish we could more easily forget our pain—but you can lose the prison of it. If you have to say "I forgive you" once a day for the next hundred days, then do it, because your next *thousand* days are worth it.

DISAPPOINTMENT WITH GOD

I'd like to acknowledge that sometimes we feel most hurt and disappointed by God. And this is quite a unique position to be in. How are we to draw near to one we feel may push us away? How are we to surrender completely to one we associate with confusion and pain? I don't for a second presume I understand every ounce of disappointment you've endured, but I do want to express two simple words that I hope will help as you journey toward wholeness and forgiveness: *I'm sorry.*

No, I'm not apologizing for God, because God stands and rules on His own. I'm simply acknowledging that you have been disappointed by Him, and I'm sorry for the pain that's caused you. I'm in this with you. God—all-loving and all-powerful—has at times confused me, because how could He allow the Midianites to circle around my life, my heart, or my family?

Two of the people I respect the most, Rob and Laura Koke, mentored me at the first church I ever worked. And it was a joy to serve the Lord under their leadership and direction. Rob and Laura had started the church in the '90s, and it grew and influenced thousands of lives. My life was one of those. I received so much encouragement, vision, and insight from them both. It's from Rob and Laura Koke that I learned in such a beautiful way how to be a pastor and continue to lean into my family. It's from Rob and Laura that I saw the importance of attending my kids' games, scheduling date nights, holding family prayer time, and laughing together around the dinner table.

In July 2009, something unthinkable happened to Rob and Laura Koke. Their middle son, seventeen-year-old Caleb, fell asleep at the wheel, veered off the road, hit a tree, and in an instant went from life on this earth to looking at Jesus face-to-face. I remember getting the phone call that Caleb was no longer with us. I remember walking into Rob and Laura's home and hugging them. I watched them grieve in the days that followed, and these two warriors and heart-broken parents taught me this phrase: *Don't exchange what you do know for what you don't know in a time of pain.*

They knew that God is all-loving. Not partially loving, not somewhat loving, but completely and totally the embodiment of love. And the same glorious Creator, who has graciously called Himself our Father, is also all-powerful, with the ability to hold the entire universe in the palm of His hand. So they chose to hold on to these facts about God that they did know, even in light of such tragedy and confusion. And one day, they will see Caleb again. Though that hope is glorious, the waiting is still painful. But they continue to preach the good news of Jesus Christ with passion, zeal, and conviction—and somehow the pain of what they walk through makes their message that much more believable.

Again, I don't want to trivialize your pain or what you've experienced, but neither do I want you to miss out on all that's in front of you because of the pain that's behind you. Perhaps you need to close this book for a moment and talk with God. But before you go, please remember that your under-the-oak moments aren't just about you. Your moment may very well intersect with another's and be essential in helping someone walk through their moment of crisis. So hold on to the truth of God's love and power, and let go of the disappointment and confusion. If you can't do this for yourself, maybe you can for the sake of those who need you.

PRIDE

Pride is a killer of all good things. It blocks you from the precious and meaningful moments of life.

And pride is sneaky because when you're being prideful, you don't always realize it. That's how pride is able to slither its way into even the best of us.

You've heard the story of David and Goliath. You know, the young shepherd boy who faced a huge giant and defeated him with a slingshot.[5] That was a massive moment in the life of David—a moment that catapulted him to a place of influence and affected generations. Do you know how he ended up at the scene of the battle? His dad told him to take lunch to his brothers, who were soldiers in Israel's army. That's right—David was delivering DoorDash to his brothers. An order of Chick-fil-A sent by his father. And it was when delivering the meal that David heard the taunts of the giant that he would defeat.

What if David had said to his father, "I don't do food deliveries. Sorry, Dad. Find someone else to do that menial task. I'm too good for that. I've got bigger things in store for my future"? Imagine how pride could've kept him from where God was taking him. What job or role or position do you think is beneath you? What is it you just won't do? That may be the very thing you must do to meet your moment under the oak.

Even if the task in front of you isn't what you are gifted or wired to do, I encourage you to do it nonetheless.

I love being a dad. Becoming one was what I dreamed of when I was a young man. At fifteen or sixteen, I was looking forward to being a husband and a father one day. (I also wanted to be an astronaut and the president of the United States. Though now Elon Musk is trying to get us to Mars, and I plan on staying fully grounded on Earth. I also don't think I'm supposed to run for president, but I'll let you know if anything changes. Ha!) When our kids came home from the hospital, it was on! By *on*, I mean massive amounts of love and a lack of sleep. Those two things were so real. Eventually our kids got on a great sleep schedule, but until that time—wow, it was rough. Talk about being delirious. Talk about being irritable. Talk about being madly in love. All of it was true at the same time.

I didn't need to be gifted to change diapers. I needed to change diapers because my kids were pooping themselves and my beautiful wife was doing everything she could to feed these amazing humans. I had to play my part, and if it was diapers, then it was diapers. If it meant waking up at 3:17 A.M., holding a crying baby, and trusting God to give this child just a little bit of peace so that my lovely wife could have a few moments of rest, so be it. That's what needed to be done. I did not say to my wife, "I don't do diapers. I don't do nighttime baby-holding. I only play with the child when the child is happy and fully content." As difficult as the sleepless nights were, those were the moments that God gave me to bond with my children.

The principle is true no matter what task is before you. There are things in life that we're asked to do that are inconvenient, outside of our skill set, or a mix of both, but they play a huge part in preparing us for the moments that God has set aside for us. Again, we don't know when our moments are coming. And we don't want pride to blind us from what God is trying to bring to us. You might need to ask yourself, a trusted friend, or a mentor if there's something that you've written off or been unwilling to do that is hindering you from the place God wants to take you.

Some of us don't realize that our own unwillingness is pride. When people say they want to be entrepreneurs, I love it. But I also wonder if they know what it takes. When you start a business, usually other people aren't around to do the things you don't want to do. *You* have to do all the things—whether you like them or not—so that one day the company can grow and you can focus on the tasks you want to do. Don't let pride steal the moment God has for you.

One of my favorite Bible characters is John the Baptist, a prophet and teacher. His message was not a soft one at all. He was confrontational, he dressed crazy, and he ate some interesting things, but his popularity was well-documented.[6] In fact, people wondered if he was the Messiah. I don't know how popular you were in high school or in college, but I'm sure no one has ever called you the Messiah. Yet John the Baptist had people asking him this very real question: "Are you the Messiah we've been looking for?" John the Baptist didn't let all this praise and applause and attention go to his head. He didn't leverage this attention to somehow elevate himself. He understood his mission to prepare the way for the true Messiah, who was actually his cousin Jesus. John the Baptist said something along the lines of "One mightier than I is coming. I can't even tie His Jordans. He's going to baptize you with the Holy Spirit and with fire."[7] John the Baptist kept pointing people to Jesus. And he said these words (my favorite verse in all of the Bible) in John 3:30: "[Jesus] must become greater; I must become less."

I ask God to make that my heart's cry as well—that Jesus would become greater and I would become less. I pray this not just so I don't miss my moments, but also because I want my life to be for the glory and the fame and the name of my Savior.

But there is, without a doubt, a benefit to me personally as I live this way, and it's not material things. The benefit is a soul that can receive with purity what God has set aside for me. I can love my wife and my family and my church and my friends the way God has called me to. My eyes aren't so focused on myself that I miss the moments God has for me to be a source of strength for others.

Pride is a killer. And it's a sneaky one. I have to make sure I don't unintentionally allow it to slip into my humility. But I don't spend too much time on these mental gymnastics. I try to spend more time on my knees in worship and prayer, more time serving and loving others, more time asking my wife, my kids, and those close to me, "How am I doing?" Then I allow the Holy Spirit to show me where I might be off, where I might be focused on the wrong things. But I don't get so overwhelmed with messing up that I miss out on living my life for the glory of God. I pivot and grow.

As we prepare for the moments God has for us, let's not be so concerned about missing them that we miss the God of the moments. Let's be sure we keep our eyes fixed in the right place so that we are celebrating and gazing on the beauty of our Savior, recognizing that He is doing a profound work in the world and through us. He has called us, by His grace, to partner with Him to accomplish His will "on earth as it is in heaven."[8]

Resting in our God-given, intrinsic value with gratitude and humility is key to recognizing and receiving the moments when the God of the universe shows up under a random oak tree and wants to use our lives to bring hope, life, and strength to others. I know He doesn't want to do that only with my life. God wants to do that with your life as well.

3
THE STRENGTH YOU HAVE

My kids are convinced that money grows on trees. I've received birthday and Christmas wish lists that made me look at them like they'd lost their minds.

A pony
A dog
A lightsaber
A car
A minivan (not happening)
An apple tree
An iPhone
A PS36 (there isn't one yet, but it's coming)

As ridiculous as these requests are, there's something wonderful about them: Our kids think we can actually provide these things. They aren't thinking about the price tags; they're thinking about how they've seen us provide in the past. They are so secure in our love for them each child feels the freedom to ask for all the gifts they can imagine. But that's not always the case between us and God.

"Pardon me, my lord," Gideon replied, "but if the Lord is with us, why has all this happened to us? Where are all his wonders that our ancestors told us about when they said, 'Did not the Lord bring us up out of Egypt?' But now the Lord has abandoned us and given us into the hand of Midian."

The Lord turned to him and said, "Go in the strength you have and save Israel out of Midian's hand. Am I not sending you?"

"Pardon me, my lord," Gideon replied, "but how can I save Israel? My clan is the weakest in Manasseh, and I am the least in my family."

The Lord answered, "I will be with you, and you will strike down all the Midianites, leaving none alive." (Judges 6:13–16)

Gideon had lost hope in the strength of God. *Where are all His wonders . . . ?* Gideon might as well be a kid with no birthday wish list because he doesn't think anything good is going to come. Nothing will be given—no hope, no strength, no victory, no breakthrough, no change. He's polite in his unbelief: "Pardon me, my lord." It has a bit of a British accent to it. Maybe he gave a bow. And you and I, we do this all the time.

"Pardon me, Lord, but why have I struggled this long?"

"Pardon me, Lord, but if You're good, why did this bad thing happen?"

"Pardon me, Lord, but I trusted You in the past and it didn't work out."

Polite unbelief is still unbelief. And it's this lack of trust in the character of God that hinders Gideon—and us—from seeing what God wants to do in and through him.

Polite unbelief is still unbelief.

Unfortunately, my dad wasn't as present in my life as I wanted him to be or as he wanted to be. I love my dad; our relationship is now restored. But his inconsistency in my life created an obstacle in my walk with God. The minutes I sat on the front porch, waiting for my dad to pick me up but only to be let down, and the times he promised wonderful things but didn't come through—those moments distorted my understanding of God. I thought if I were good enough, my dad would always show up. So I became a man who thought his performance was the way to procure the love of a father. And the love of *the Father.* I came to believe you have to earn grace. There's no forgiveness; you have to be perfect.

I didn't realize this until I learned to process my emo-

tions (thanks to my beautiful wife) and sat with some phe-
nomenal mentors and leaders. These people helped me
realize the pain from my childhood was creating a wall between God and me. So I'm not upset with Gideon for asking
hard questions. He is me, and he is you. When you've had
years of disappointment and then someone announces, "The
LORD is with you, mighty warrior,"[1] there is a tension between the words you hear and the reality you've experienced. And for many of us, the realities of life have
overshadowed the words of God. So Gideon asked the question we all ask: "If what You're saying is true, then why have
I experienced something different?" Thank you, Gideon, for
saying what so many of us have been thinking.

Gideon had heard stories of God's protection and provision: "Our ancestors told us about when . . . the LORD
[brought] us up out of Egypt."[2] Do you know the story
Gideon referenced? (The long version is in Exodus 3–14.)
God picked a people through whom He would love, redeem,
and bless the world. He did not choose them because of
their awesomeness but because of His own awesomeness.
The people God picked became slaves in Egypt. For years.
Like four hundred years. They prayed to the Lord over that
entire time to free them.

Eventually, God sent Moses, a man who was born to Hebrew parents and then adopted by the pharaoh's daughter.
Moses went to Pharaoh and said on behalf of God, "Let my
people go!" Pharaoh said no. There were financial, spiritual,
and emotional reasons he said no. Then God sent ten
plagues that ravaged the slave masters. The last one was a
devastating blow, causing the death of the firstborn in every

Egyptian household. At last, Pharaoh let God's kids go. They left slavery with treasure: gold, silver, and Air Jordan 1s. But just as they left Egypt, Pharaoh changed his mind and ordered his army to chase after them. When the Israelites got to the Red Sea, God miraculously parted it, and they walked across on dry ground, but the Egyptian army was swallowed up in the water.

Those were just *some* of the miracles Gideon was referring to. And he asked the Lord, "Where are those miracles? Where's the liberation? Because right now, I'm living in fear. Right now, I can't keep my head above water. Right now, I feel forgotten. I feel angry. I'm not fine living like this. I don't like it. But what's worse is living with the disappointment of a God I can't count on."

> I know you have your reasons to not believe, but God has His reasons to believe in you.

Yet God always interrupts our disappointments with a bigger agenda. And today God might be interrupting you. I pray you sense the Lord talking to you right now. Hear Him graciously reminding you to dream again, believe again, trust Him again. God still has the ability to do more than you can ask or imagine.[3] His overwhelming love is stronger than the reasons you thought it better to play it safe. I know you have your reasons to not believe, but God has His reasons for placing gifts and purpose in you.

Imagine you and I are sitting next to each other, and without you knowing it, I deposit one hundred dollars in your Venmo account. A few minutes later, I ask you for seventy-five dollars. You tell me, "I don't have seventy-five dollars." But you're wrong—you just haven't seen the notification yet. Since you don't know what I gave you, you think I'm a fool to ask you for it. But *I know what I gave you.*

Before Gideon ever took a breath, God put in him gifts of leadership and strategy. He slipped Gideon a hundred dollars before Gideon was even walking. And now, all these years later, God is asking for Gideon to put to use what He gave him in the first place. The demand seems ludicrous to Gideon. But it makes all the sense in the world to God. Our loving, all-powerful Savior talks to us from the perspective of our destiny, but we talk to Him from the perspective of our deficiencies.

Remember, this conversation with Gideon involved him, but it did not *revolve* around him. This was an assignment *from* God to rescue His people. This was not *all about* Gideon.

Full disclosure: I was intimidated about writing this book. God has called me a mighty warrior, called me to serve His kids in a new way. And I know clearly the 45,986 reasons I should not write a book. (I could list them all here, but I'll spare you the details.) The thing is, this book involves me, but it doesn't revolve around me. It's about God and serving and helping God's kids. So it is with every endeavor, great and small, that God places in front of you. Volunteering at church, giving a generous gift, helping a neighbor, starting a business or nonprofit, painting a picture, giving advice to a friend, or running for office. It involves you but does not revolve around you.

But all Gideon could see was his pain. He said, "The LORD has abandoned us."⁴ Wow.

Once again, I appreciate Gideon's honesty. I appreciate our honesty about what we're going through. But, friends, this tension is keeping us locked away and hidden.

The question is, Can you move beyond the tension and your disappointment and sit with a young person, a community, a family, or a nation and open yourself up so you can share what God placed in you for them? That's what this book is. It's God opening me up to serve and help others like me. I pray we never allow our feelings to thwart what God wants to do in us and through us.

God's response to Gideon's honest disappointment is "Go in the strength you have and save Israel out of Midian's hand. Am I not sending you?"⁵

How could God say this in response to Gideon's feelings of abandonment? Because God made Gideon. God knew what was placed in Gideon better than Gideon knew himself. God was essentially saying, "I have already acted on your behalf. I have already prepared you." He is speaking the same thing over your life today.

Am I not sending you to that school? Go in the strength you have.

Am I not sending you to that community? Go in the strength you have.

Am I not calling you to parenthood? Go in the strength you have.

Am I not sending you to that job, that city, that nation? Go in the strength you have.

Am I not sending you to solve that problem with what I gave you when I knit you in your mother's womb?[6] Go in the strength you have.

I have talked to many people over the years who believe there's a particular reason why God can't use them. Gideon had a specific reason in his mind also—in fact, he had two: "My clan is the weakest in Manasseh, and I am the least in my family."[7] No one who looked like Gideon had accomplished what God was asking of him.

We have our two points too:

> My past is a mess *and* so is my family.
> I've made terrible mistakes *and* my bank account is empty.
> I've never been popular *and* people don't seem to get me.

But the truth is, there is *no* situation or reason that can disqualify you from being used for God's glory.

I remember God gave us a dream (a literal dream) to start a church that would look like Revelation 7:9–10:

> There before me was a great multitude that no one could count, from every nation, tribe, people and language, standing before the throne and before the Lamb. They were wearing white robes and were holding palm branches in their hands. And they cried out in a loud voice:

"Salvation belongs to our God,
who sits on the throne,
and to the Lamb."

But there was a problem in my mind. Both Oneka and I are Black. Yep, 110 percent African American. To the bone! And we didn't know of another Black couple leading a church that looked like heaven. Black people went to predominately Black churches. White people went to predominately White churches. Latino people went to predominately Latino churches. Asian people went to predominately Asian churches. Old people went to predominately old people churches. Young people went to predominately young people churches. We don't think there is anything inherently wrong with this social norm. It just wasn't the dream we were going after.

We knew Black people would follow a Black pastor, but would other ethnic groups? In America, we don't have to look far to see the stains and sins of racism in our land.

I told God, "You are giving us a dream, a call, a purpose. But I don't know if You've taken into account *who* it is You're asking to do this."

Eighteen months after that dream, we launched Shoreline City Church in Dallas with our two sons and about six people. A church grew that looked like heaven on earth: people from all backgrounds. Now people walk into our church and are blown away at what God has done. No matter the location you visit, it's a beautiful picture of heaven on earth. But I hadn't really seen it before, so I didn't know if God could do it.

What has God called you to do? And what are your two reasons it can't happen?

Why do you think God got it wrong with you?

For some of us, two reasons doesn't cut it because we have a whole book full of reasons why God can't use us.

Please understand, my friend, God took your reasons into account before you did. He knew what He was working with when He called you. Your faults and excuses were accounted for. But His love and the finished work of the cross of Christ are greater, and His grace equation has come out with a positive answer. God knows this and believes it. Now you need to believe it too.

God didn't put you on this earth for safety and security; He didn't place you here to be your version of perfect. He put you on this earth for His purpose and His glory! So let these words resonate deep in your soul:

The Lord is with you, mighty warrior.

4

THE ESSENTIALS YOU NEED

Starting a new journey can be incredibly daunting, especially if you've been in one place for a while. You get used to the scenery, the situation, the flow. My wife and I first lived in Tulsa, Oklahoma. It's where we got our start, made wonderful friends, and found our flow.

We were married in 1997. Yeah, that's right. That may seem like four hundred years ago to some of you, but to us, it seems like just yesterday. Our wedding was in a stunning Methodist church, one we could not afford to get married in, but we were shown favor by the pastor.

I played basketball at the university we attended, and our team had a banquet at this church. My wife was with me (we were newly engaged then), and we both loved the auditorium. It had a gorgeous balcony, a pipe organ, and lovely deep brown woodwork. The ceilings were incredibly expansive, and the pews were wrapped in velvet. Oneka and I thought this would be a great place to get married, but we doubted we could afford it. I sent a note to the pastor, Dr. Tom Wilson, and asked him what it would cost for us to get married at his beautiful church.

Dr. Wilson said, "Earl, it was so wonderful to have you and the rest of the basketball team there at our church. How about you get married here for five hundred dollars?" Now, mind you, Oneka and I were broke. We were college students, and we didn't come from families with deep pockets. When we heard "five hundred dollars," it still felt like a lot of money. But we knew this was considerably less than the usual fee, so we jumped on it and could not believe we were getting such a beautiful venue.

After a gorgeous ceremony, we lived in Tulsa for those years and had so many game nights with friends. As a matter of fact, we had a bunch of young couple friends. We stayed up late—all of us, two incomes, no kids—living the life. It was the greatest time in the world.

Then came a moment when God called us and opened the door to go to Austin, Texas. We were excited about the new opportunity, but it required us to leave Tulsa. We had to leave our friends, our community, and all we had known, and step into the unknown. We had been incredibly excited about the life God had given us in Tulsa. We had married and purchased our first home there. But now God was taking us to Austin.

So we packed up a U-Haul, attached the car we had named Hannah to the back, and started our journey, a brand-new adventure. Oneka wanted to continue her broadcast-journalism career and was seeking a job at the NBC, ABC, or CBS station in town. I was going to work for a wonderful, life-giving church.

But the move brought a big adjustment. Suddenly, we didn't know anyone. We didn't have a crew of people to go out with on the weekends. We didn't have years of history with anyone. We were excited about the season but definitely felt we were in a new place. After some time, things began to change. Friendships and community blossomed. Long-term relationships formed. Doors opened to enable us to grow and mature. We learned what it meant to be a husband and wife working in a local church setting. It was all new, it was a change, but, wow, there was favor.

And I know it wasn't just favor; it was God's presence that went with us.

The start of any journey can feel unnerving, but we don't need to forge ahead empty-handed. There are three things that are essential for the road ahead: God's presence, His power, and His favor. Because, friends, we are about to take this turn with Gideon from doubt to belief, from insecurity to confidence, from self-disqualification to God-equipped.

GOD'S PRESENCE

God is not calling us to a life of adventure and purpose apart from His presence. No—in fact, He is calling us to lean into His presence. He wants us to understand that apart from Him, we can do nothing.[1] Please understand—and this has to be so clear in your heart and mind—you and I are not so gifted that we can accomplish the purpose of God without the presence of God. We need His presence. We need God to be with us and in us and over us. We need Him to surround us and fill us.

> You and I are not so gifted that we can accomplish the purpose of God without the presence of God.

In Exodus 3, we see Moses wrestling with his call. He wasn't sure he could move forward, that he had what it would take to accomplish what God had put in front of him. And again, God promised His presence: "I will be with you."[2]

My grandparents were and still are my heroes. They had been married for more than sixty years when my grandfather transitioned from this life to the next and saw our glorious Savior face-to-face. My grandmother is holding on and has celebrated one hundred years on this earth.

When I was a kid, I spent my summers in New Jersey with them. They were incredibly godly people—not perfect, but godly. They would show up at church early and stay late. They were part of the same Lutheran church for over fifty years. I first had communion at their church, and it was real wine. I still remember coughing incessantly as I downed it at twelve years old. Now we use grape juice in our church.

But that's where I spent my summers with my grand-parents. They lived out in the country, where the only real light at night is the moon and the stars. While I was staying with them, I went to a friend's house late one night, and we foolishly watched a horror movie. This was back in the days of *A Nightmare on Elm Street*. We watched Freddy devour and destroy everything. We shouted at the TV, jumped when we needed to jump, and grabbed each other by the shirt—laughing and terrified all at the same time. But the problem was, after the movie, I had to walk home to my grandparents. Yep, walk home on those dark country roads with only the light of the heavens guiding my way. Can I tell y'all I was petrified? Do you know what it's like to be a thirteen-year-old who just watched a horror movie and has to walk past a cornfield and woods? I could hear the crickets and frogs, and a still, small breeze washed over my body, keeping me just cold enough to shiver. Every owl that hooted made me whip my head around so fast.

I swore there was somebody behind me. I was sure eyes were peering out from the bushes, and I promise you, Freddy was after me. I tried to act tough initially. I walked slowly, telling myself it was just a movie. But eventually the fear got to me, and I took off running as fast as I possibly could to my grandparents' house. Let me tell you, if there had been a track-and-field coach watching me, they would've asked my mom to release me from middle school to train in the mountains of Colorado because it sure looked like I was destined to be an Olympic sprinter.

But I felt a lot different on another night walking to my grandparents' house after a movie, when there were five or six of us together. Being in the presence of my friends, I had a higher level of confidence. Honestly, we were just messing around and probably laughing at inappropriate jokes. But all the while, I wasn't as concerned about the cornfields and the bushes and the sounds of the owls and the crickets.

Presence changes perspective.

Presence changes how we walk from one place to another.

Presence changes our level of confidence and security.

Whether it's moving from one city to another or one season to another, presence makes a world of difference. I pray God's presence becomes so real as we walk through life with Him by our side that we will trust we have all we need to enjoy the journey.

GOD'S POWER

In Judges 6:16, God said to Gideon, "I will be with you, and you will strike down all the Midianites, leaving none alive."

Gideon was tasked with a new plan, and he would have to take some significant steps of faith. God told him to mount an offensive attack against the raiding Midianites. And what would he need to move forward?

God said (my paraphrase), "Gideon, I'm going to give you My presence and My power to accomplish the call I gave you while you were still in your mother's womb. I want you to understand, Gideon, not only do you need My presence, but also you need My power."[3]

You see, the power of God is what enables us to do the

thing He has called us to do. In order to accomplish a God-sized dream, you and I need God-sized power. It is foolish for us to think we can accomplish what He is asking us to do void of His power. It would be like an electric car trying to move forward without first getting a charge. The beautiful thing is that God promises us His power.

> The supernatural power of the risen Savior is running through your actual body. The power you need to be faithful and bold is the natural by-product of your surrender to the authority of Jesus.

The Bible tells us in Romans 8:11, "If the Spirit of him who raised Jesus from the dead is living in you, he who raised Christ from the dead will also give life to your mortal bodies because of his Spirit who lives in you." The supernatural power of the risen Savior is running through your actual body. The power you need to be faithful and bold is the natural by-product of your surrender to the authority of Jesus. We aren't the source of power. Jesus is! The resurrected Savior has made a way for each of us to live in His power.

GOD'S FAVOR

Favor opens doors you cannot open. Favor gives you opportunities you never could have manufactured in and of yourself. Favor puts you in rooms you don't deserve to be in or didn't think you could be in. It gives you a voice you didn't think you could ever have.

The reality is that you and I have experienced favor we thought was because we were so good, so skilled, so deserving. But favor finds God at its source. It's God's kindness that leads us to repentance.[4] If the bad things don't get our attention, God will use good things to get our attention. Acts 14:17 tells us, "[God] has shown kindness by giving you rain from heaven and crops in their seasons; he provides you with plenty of food and fills your hearts with joy."

I mentioned already that my basketball coach in college was Hall of Famer Bill Self. At the time of this writing, he is on a lifelong contract with the University of Kansas. But I first met Coach Self in a Subway sandwich shop. I'm not kidding. This is documented all over the internet because anytime Coach Self finds himself in the Final Four or in a championship game in the NCAA tournament, somehow a reporter gets ahold of me and asks how we met.

I played basketball at a small high school, and it gave me so many opportunities. And can I just tell you? There was favor there. Somebody actually paid for me to go to that private school and get a fantastic education. To this day, I still don't know who it was.

But although there was so much favor there, the small school didn't get me any offers to play basketball in college. A few colleges sent letters but nothing significant.

I headed to Oral Roberts University, which has a Division I basketball program—the highest level of basketball for a collegiate athlete. And I wanted to play, but I wasn't recruited. I was determined to try out and hopefully make the team. Then, one random day, I stepped across the street from the university to pick up a foot-long sandwich at Subway, and in walked Coach Bill Self with two of the coaching staff. I was already a fanboy, so I recognized him right away.

The way he tells the story is that I introduced myself and said "sir" about thirty-seven times in a two-minute conversation.

"Hello, sir. My name is Earl, sir. Sir, I'd love to play basketball for your team, sir. Sir, how do I go about playing for your team, sir, if you would not mind, sir?"

That's how he tells the story. And that's how we met. A little bit later, Coach Self walked up to me on campus and said, "Hey, I hear you can play a little basketball. Would you like to come down and play with the team?" I went and played some pickup games, and I was on the team from that day until I graduated from college.

Favor. I can't make that up. It was not something I manufactured. I didn't know Coach Self ate Subway sandwiches. I didn't know other members of the basketball team were talking to Coach Self about me, telling him there was a kid on campus who could play a little ball and should probably play with them. That's favor. I didn't know my saying "sir" thirty-seven times in a two-minute conversation was going to make an impression on him and put a smile on his face. I didn't know any of these things. All I knew was that I wanted to play basketball in college, and God was the one who showed favor and opened the doors.

Presence, power, favor. Gideon needed all three to move forward, and so do you. There will be many blessings that come your way, and I ask you not to chalk them up to your strength and your determination. Yes, it matters that we work hard and try. Yes, it matters that we knock on doors. Yes, it matters that we give our full effort and energy to accomplish what God is asking us to do. But please understand, if it's a God-sized dream, it will also require God-sized favor.

I needed favor to make it on the basketball team as a walk-on in college, to be voted team captain three out of the four years that I was a player. And I need favor even to this day. I need favor with my wife. I need favor with my kids. I need favor with the people God has called me to lead. I need favor with people I haven't met yet, and so do you.

We need favor. We need doors to be opened for us that only God can open. That's what God's favor does, and that's what Gideon needed in order to move forward.

As we continue our journey with Gideon and we see his life mirroring ours, we're beginning to see that the presence of God is with us, His power is with us, and, yes, His favor is upon us.

Presence, power, favor. All three are promised to Gideon and also given to us—not for our glory or fame, but to accomplish what God has put us on this earth to do for His glory, to reach His people with the salvation found in the death, burial, and resurrection of Jesus Christ.

5
DO IT SCARED

About halfway through the conversation with the angel of the Lord, Gideon finally realizes who it is he's talking to. And this conversation is about to change his life. This conversation will change his family and an entire group of people in a deeply powerful way. Let's pick up the story again in Judges 6:22–24:

> When Gideon realized that it was the angel of the LORD, he exclaimed, "Alas, Sovereign LORD! I have seen the angel of the LORD face to face!"
>
> But the LORD said to him, "Peace! Do not be afraid. You are not going to die."
>
> So Gideon built an altar to the LORD there

and called it The LORD Is Peace. To this day it
stands in Ophrah of the Abiezrites.

Many theologians say that the angel of the Lord was not
just an angel, because Gideon calls Him Lord. And not only
was He the Lord, but they believe this was actually Jesus
showing up in the Old Testament. This was Jesus making a
guest appearance, if you will. And when Gideon realizes
that this is the Lord, he is terrified.

We have lost honor and reverence for who Jesus is and
have become so flippant with Him that we don't understand
that He is supremely powerful and mighty and otherworldly.
His very presence and power are enough to melt a mountain like wax, to melt us like wax. But He chooses to extend
His kindness and His grace, and we are not consumed when
we could be. Gideon realized, coming face-to-face with God,
Oh my goodness, I could die. But God brings life. "Peace!" He
says to Gideon. "Do not be afraid. You are not going to
die."[1]

As you move forward in what God is calling you to do,
you need this peace. You need "the peace of God, which
transcends all understanding."[2] You need a quiet soul and
steady mind so you don't think everything is up to you.
Peace. As Judges 6:24 tells us, "The LORD Is Peace."

The Lord is peace.

If you're anything like me, you get anxious when the
task before you is bigger than you. So, let these words wash
over your anxious soul and mind. The Lord is peace for you
today. The Lord is peace for you tomorrow. The Lord is
peace when you feel confident, and the Lord is peace when

you feel insecure. The Lord is peace when you have all the hope in the world, and the Lord is peace when you feel abandoned, isolated, and lost. The Lord is peace when you are applying to grad school, and the Lord is peace when you're waiting for the response. The Lord is peace in singleness, and the Lord is peace in marriage.

And because the Lord is peace and His presence is with you, you also have peace.

When Jesus and His disciples were crossing the Sea of Galilee, a storm hit the boat and the disciples were terrified. Jesus stepped forward, and He said, "Quiet! Be still!"[3]

The disciples were amazed that He was able to control the wind and the waves with just His voice. But we don't have to be all that surprised, because He's the one that made the wind and the waves in the first place, because the whole universe is held together by Jesus, as Colossians teaches us.[4] And Jesus spoke over that storm, "Peace."

"Let the peace of Christ rule in [our] hearts,"[5] because you and I are about to embark on a journey that will stretch and challenge us in significant ways. We are about to face some seemingly insurmountable obstacles. God is going to ask us to tear down these barriers, and some of them will be incredibly personal.

TEAR DOWN THE ALTARS

I was nine years old, maybe ten, in the back seat of the car with my friend Tommy, taking a trip from Providence to Boston to see the Red Sox play. My dad and Tommy's dad were in the front seats. Tommy was named after his dad, and I was named after mine.

I was behind the driver's seat, and Tommy was behind the passenger seat, riding in my father's yellow Cadillac Seville. I looked down at my feet, and I saw a magazine underneath my father's chair. I reached down and pulled it out. It was a *Penthouse* magazine, filled with pictures of naked women. I felt a rush of energy as Tommy and I flipped through the pages, looking at these images, thinking our dads didn't see us. I found out years later that they had known exactly what we were doing, but unfortunately, they didn't stop us. And it was in that moment that a terrible altar was built in my life—the altar of pornography—which created guilt and secrecy and negatively affected my walk with God and, years later, my relationship with my wife.

When I was a young adult in college, God asked me to tear down that idol. "Earl, go back to when you were ten years old—you were looking at that magazine, blown away by what you saw but not protected from the poison that was entering your heart." The desire is not what was bad; it was the timing and the focus of that desire that was an issue. The desire that God had put in me to love and care and connect with a woman at some point in my life was being distorted, polluted, and poisoned. But the grace of almighty God can cover that sin, and it can cover my father's sin of not protecting me.

Some things, if not torn down, will hunt us down.

You know, honestly, I'm not a big one for wallowing in the past. I don't like to look back all that much, but some things, if not torn down, will end up hunting us down. If you don't deal with them, they will deal with you for the rest of your life. And for a long time, I didn't deal with this altar to pornography properly. In my teenage years, though I loved Jesus and had God's favor on my life, I still found myself going back to this poison, time and time again. I'd love to tell you that in college I never looked at it, but that wouldn't be the truth. I had my times and my moments of falling back into the pit. It was an altar that hadn't been torn down.

We all have altars we need to remove, and Judges 6:25–26 shows how God helps and guides us to do just that.

> The LORD said to him, "Take the second bull from your father's herd, the one seven years old. Tear down your father's altar to Baal and cut down the Asherah pole beside it. Then build a proper kind of altar to the LORD your God on the top of this height. Using the wood of the Asherah pole that you cut down, offer the second bull as a burnt offering."

God essentially told Gideon, "I want you moving forward, and to do that, you need to deal with the altars your father built." Those altars to false gods were built on lies, insecurities, fears, doubts, and distortion. So Gideon's first mission, after surrendering his life to God, was to tear down what his father built. In order for Gideon to go forward in his calling, God was asking him to go back and confront the skeletons in his closet.

I don't know what your altar is. I don't know what your father built or what was put in front of you that you have allowed to exist. But with the presence of God and the power of God and the favor of God and the peace of God, I implore you to move forward by going back and tearing down the altar. Let's deal with it. Let's not pretend it didn't happen or that it didn't affect you—it did. Let's not pretend it hasn't messed with you—it has. Let's face it, and like Gideon, if you need to, do it scared. Judges 6:27 says,

> Gideon took ten of his servants and did as the Lord told him. But because he was afraid of his family and the townspeople, he did it at night rather than in the daytime.

Gideon took trusted servants and did as the Lord told him, but under the cover of darkness, where he had less chance of being confronted by the villagers or his own father. I used to beat myself up for being afraid while I did something God asked me to do, but I look here at Gideon, and that's exactly what he did. So even if you do it afraid, at least you're doing it.

If you're afraid to confess some things to your pastor, do it scared.

If you're afraid to deal with your past because of what it might mean for your future, do it scared.

If you're afraid to get honest with yourself about what you experienced or something you've done—whether intentionally or accidentally—or a problem that you've allowed to persist, do it scared.

Find a therapist who loves Jesus, and do it scared.

Gideon tore down the altar as God asked, and he did it scared. What is it God is asking you to do? Because, friends, we're about to forge ahead. In a few short verses, the Spirit of the Lord will come upon Gideon and he will take a huge step forward, not just for his life but for the lives of a bunch of other people, as God is going to use him to rescue a nation from oppression and difficulty.

Gideon has the presence, the power, the favor, and the peace of God, not just to accomplish what's ahead of him in the future but also to overcome and deal with what happened in the past. You see, what Jesus Christ did for us on the cross is more than enough to forgive our past. It's more than enough to cover and cleanse our past. But you and I still believe that our insecurities, failures, and faults, what we've done and what has been done to us, are somehow greater than the glorious cross and resurrection of Jesus Christ. But, my friends, that is a lie. Your sin and my sin, and the sins that others have committed against us, are not greater than what Jesus Christ has done for us on the cross.

But you and I still believe that our insecurities, failures, and faults, what we've done and what has been done to us, are somehow greater than the glorious cross and resurrection of Jesus Christ. But, my friends, that is a lie.

Allow me to remind you once again, the Lord is peace. And you have His favor, His power, and His presence. Everything that is unlike God can be torn down. Every false altar must fall. Go ahead and cut it down. Right now, in your thoughts, as you write in your journal, in this moment—cut it down. And in its place, build the proper kind of altar to the Lord.

> The kind of altar that is built on hope.
> The kind of altar that is built on belief in the
>   sovereignty and love of God.
> The kind of altar that can change an entire
>   family line.
> The kind of altar that's ultimately built by
>   grace and faith in the finished work of
>   Jesus Christ.

Pornography still tries to knock on my door. But by the presence, power, favor, and peace of God, it has been over twenty-five years since I've looked at pornography. I'm believing God for the grace every day to put one foot in front of the other so that this altar will stay torn down. But it's weird how these altars from our past somehow begin to reassemble, even though we did all the cutting. We did all the tearing down we needed to do. But then we still need grace for another day to not allow what this culture or even the Enemy of our souls, the devil, would try to bring our way.

WITH GOD

Whatever it is you need to cut down, please understand that you are not alone. God is not asking you to do something apart from Him. He'll never send you where He doesn't already abide, because that's the generous, loving, and present Savior we have. So even if you are wiping tears from your eyes, you are not wiping them alone. And if you are afraid, you are not afraid alone. And if you are fired up to take this turn and move forward and deal with all that needs to be dealt with, you are not fired up alone. You and I live lives with God, surrendered to Jesus, and filled with the Holy Spirit.

It's imperative we recognize that our acts of faith don't just affect us; they also influence those who are watching.

If you've ever been cliff jumping, you'll already know a little about the power of watching others take courageous leaps. I had never been cliff jumping until college. A bunch of my friends and I went to Lake Tenkiller (pronounced *teen-killer*—why I decided to go cliff jumping at a lake with said name can only be chalked up to the stupidity of youth). There were what looked like hundred-foot cliffs (they were actually twenty to forty feet high), and all afternoon we lay in the sun and ate food, and my friends jumped off the cliffs into the deep lake. I went along, but I was *not* going to jump. No way! I'm a decent swimmer, but it made no sense to leave the perfectly good ground to soar through the air into the abyss of the lake. Quite simply, I was afraid. But every friend jumped. Guys. Girls. People I thought would never do it. It sounds simple, but their courage inspired me.

This is one of the many powerful ripple effects of doing what you know is right even when you're afraid: You will inevitably and sometimes unknowingly inspire others to tear down their own altars. Your courage—to stay married, volunteer, forgive, start the business, or let go of something you thought would last forever—actually encourages (meaning, "to put courage in") another to take the step.

Our lives have never ultimately been about us. Our lives are for God, His story, and the people He's called us to reach. Tear down the altars, even if you have to do it scared. Because right now, they are standing in the way of your purpose . . . and someone else's purpose. We need your Spirit-inspired courage. We need you to get your spirit back!

6

A HOLY MISSION

My first car was a 1982 Toyota Starlet. It was the smallest car ever, had a wooden bumper, and was a stick shift. (It's still a source of pride that I can handle a clutch—something my children may never understand.) This car was a great first car. I doubt it cost more than seven bucks. I exaggerate, but you get the drift.

After a cold night in New England, leaving my friend's house, I stepped out to start this beaten-down hunk of metal and nothing happened. The car was dead. My friend's dad knew a thing or two about cars with a stick shift. You can give a manual car a good enough push and "pop the clutch" to start the car. But the car must first be pushed. It has to have movement and momentum. If it's sitting still, the car won't start. But if you get enough momentum, voilà! The car starts.

Well, we pushed. And since the car was the size of a toddler's Matchbox car, we got some great motion. Then we popped the clutch, and the car was going!

This is similar to our spiritual lives. We were sitting in our sin like a car with a dead battery. Then the Holy Spirit came along and began to push us. We were pushed toward repentance, the Cross, and the road less traveled. Then we popped the clutch (that's our faith in Jesus), and—*boom*— our car that was dead not only started moving but came alive.

I know every analogy breaks down at some point. But let me write this as clearly and succinctly as possible: The Holy Spirit is necessary for what you are being called to do. We *must* respond to the push. There is no movement without the push.

Gideon had been met by God under the oak. He'd given his excuses, torn down his altars, and now, in Judges 6:33– 35, he takes another step into his destiny and calling.

All the Midianites, Amalekites and other eastern peoples joined forces and crossed over the Jordan and camped in the Valley of Jezreel. Then the Spirit of the LORD came on Gideon, and he blew a trumpet, summoning the Abiezrites to follow him. He sent messengers throughout Manasseh, calling them to arms, and also into Asher, Zebulun and Naphtali, so that they too went up to meet them.

The Spirit of the Lord came on Gideon. Some people are uncomfortable talking about the Holy Spirit, but any person who would look at the Bible honestly can see not only the fingerprints of the Holy Spirit but the necessity of the Holy Spirit.

First and foremost, we believe in the triune God: God the Father, God the Son, God the Holy Spirit. This shows up in the first verses of the Bible, Genesis 1:1–3: "In the beginning God created the heavens and the earth. Now the earth was formless and empty, darkness was over the surface of the deep, and the *Spirit* of God was hovering over the waters. And God said, 'Let there be light,' and there was light" (emphasis mine).

At the very beginning, we see God, we see the Spirit, and we see Jesus, the Word of God, through whom everything was created.[1]

When Jesus was baptized by His cousin John in the Jordan River, "the Holy Spirit descended on him in bodily form like a dove," and God spoke powerful words over Him: "You are my Son, whom I love; with you I am well pleased."[2]

Perhaps some of us have never quite seen the Holy Spirit as an integral part of our walk with Christ. I am praying that changes today. The Holy Spirit is the gift we have been given[3]—not an it, not a what, but a *who*—to empower us to live our lives for the glory of God. The Holy Spirit—living in us—works in us so we become a reflection of His name, His fame, His glory, His goodness, and His character on the earth.

The Spirit of the Lord came on Gideon. Gideon was about to accomplish a major task. He was on the precipice of

rallying tens of thousands of soldiers to release his people
from bondage. He was on the verge of being used by the
Almighty to do a work in his generation. And before that
happened, not only were the presence, power, favor, and
peace of God given to him—not only was he asked to tear
down his father's altars—but the Spirit of God came on
him. Friends, we can't skip over this fact. Gideon needed the
Spirit of the Lord, and so do you and I. If the Spirit of the
Lord was present in the creation of the earth, why would we
think the Spirit of the Lord is not present in this moment,
in what God is doing in and through our lives?

The Spirit of the Lord came upon Jesus when He was
baptized. And John the Baptist said Jesus would baptize
with this same Holy Spirit and with fire.[4] My friends, the
Spirit of the Lord is not someone we run from; He is someone we open ourselves up to because He has been there from
the beginning and will be there into eternity. I want to give
us a little more theology around the Holy Spirit for just a
moment. We must settle in our hearts His importance and
necessity.

THE GIFT OF THE HOLY SPIRIT

Acts 1 records a conversation Jesus had with His followers
as they shared a meal: "On one occasion, while he was eat-
ing with them, he gave them this command: 'Do not leave
Jerusalem, but wait for the gift my Father promised, which
you have heard me speak about. For John baptized with
water, but in a few days you will be baptized with the Holy

Spirit. . . . But you will receive power when the Holy Spirit comes on you; and you will be my witnesses in Jerusalem, and in all Judea and Samaria, and to the ends of the earth."[5] Do you see that our Savior told His disciples—commanded them—not to leave Jerusalem but to wait for the gift that His Father promised and that Jesus Himself had spoken about?

> **It is the power of the Holy Spirit in the life of a believer, forming us and shaping us into the character and image of Christ.**

The Word, inspired by God, is true and right. And it is in this Word that we read the Holy Spirit is a gift. You and I can't be saved without the work of the Spirit. We can't be the leaders God calls us to be at home, school, or work without the Holy Spirit. It is the power of the Holy Spirit in our lives as believers that forms us and shapes us into the character and image of Christ. And the Holy Spirit is the most precious of gifts.

I'm not a big gift receiver. Presents don't move me all that much. If you've ever read *The Five Love Languages* by Gary Chapman, you understand that there are different ways people receive love, and we tend to give love in the way that we like to receive it. So if you feel loved through words of affirmation, you tend to give words of affirmation. If you like to receive love in the form of physical touch, then you tend to give love in the form of physical touch. And if you feel loved when given gifts, you tend to give gifts. My wife happens to be someone whose love language is gifts. Mine is not. So my wife likes to give me gifts, even though I don't care all that much about them.

I think my not caring about gifts came from when I was twelve years old and my mom gave me an umbrella for my birthday. She gave it to me through tears. She said, "I wanted to do so much more for you. I wanted to give you so much more, but this is all I have to give." That moment is branded on my brain—I still remember the long black umbrella, the exact place on the street where I stood with my mom as she gave me her gift, an apron tied around her waist. And I still remember her tears.

She wanted to make sure I felt loved by the gift she gave. I was very thankful and appreciative of that umbrella, but I felt love just because she was my mom. I think that might have been the moment that I decided gifts are not the measure of a person's love for you.

Fast-forward a number of years, and I'm married to an amazing, beautiful, talented woman, and one of her primary love languages is gifts. Every birthday, Christmas, and anniversary, my wife is thinking long and hard about how she is going to care for me and love me with a gift. And pretty much every single birthday, Christmas, and anniversary, she is disappointed because my responses do not match the level of effort she has put into each incredibly thoughtful gift. This has been happening for all the twenty-five years of our marriage. But there have been a few times that my wife has given me the perfect gift.

One day during 2020—the terrible year of Covid-19, when the world was shut down—a man showed up in our garage with a full weight-lifting set. And not just any weight-lifting set. A Rogue weight-lifting set. This contraption was large and metal and cool and awesome, and this gentleman set it up for me in the garage at a time when we couldn't go to the gym. I found myself in that hot garage in Dallas, Texas, doing pull-ups and incline press and dips because my wife got me the ultimate Father's Day present. It was amazing. Because we could open the garage door and basically be outside, I was even able to share it with some others, and we had our own little bubble that was working. I had friends coming over and working out with me. It was such a wonderful gift—a gift that keeps on giving over and over and over again. I know some people get a treadmill or a bike in the house and don't ever use it, but this weight-lifting set has blessed me and my sons. They got in on the fun with me. This was an amazing gift that keeps building me up every day.

The Holy Spirit is a gift that builds us up and makes us stronger. He was not given so that we can have a good church service and shout a little bit and get some goosebumps. No, my friends, the Holy Spirit was given so that we could be fashioned and formed into the image of Jesus Christ and fulfill the plans and purposes that God has for us. This is the work of the Holy Spirit.

THE HOLY SPIRIT SPEAKS

The disciples waited in Jerusalem for this gift, just as Jesus had commanded them. And, as Acts 2:1–4 says, "When the day of Pentecost came, they were all together in one place. Suddenly a sound like the blowing of a violent wind came from heaven and filled the whole house where they were sitting. They saw what seemed to be tongues of fire that separated and came to rest on each of them. All of them were filled with the Holy Spirit and began to speak in other tongues [other languages] as the Spirit enabled them."

The disciples didn't have to fake it. They didn't have to muster a response or conjure up some manufactured emotionalism. No. In this moment, when the Holy Spirit showed up, the whole house was shaken and filled. Every single person was touched. And the change did not stay in that room; it began to make its way into the streets. When you are touched by the Holy Spirit, your changed life won't stay confined to your home. What God does in the privacy of a heart explodes into the streets! And on the day of Pentecost, when Jews from all over the world were descending upon Jerusalem, they heard the praises and the glory of God in their own language. These were people from all different walks of life, and they were utterly amazed that they were hearing the praises of God in their native languages.

This, my friends, is what the Holy Spirit does in the life of a believer—He fills us. But the filling is not just for us. It is for us to be empowered to be the church in the world, to be representatives of God in our generation. Wherever you go as a follower of Jesus Christ, you go filled with the Spirit so you can speak the language of the people God has called you to reach.

When we started our church, a number of college students attended our services. It was amazing to see their lives changed and transformed by the gospel. These college students had a way of connecting with other college students that some of us "older people" may not have had. They understood the language of exams, multiple majors, wanting to not just achieve but overachieve, being involved in sports while trying to juggle schoolwork. Their peers were able to hear and see the glory of God in a unique way because they heard it from people who spoke their language. This is what the Holy Spirit does.

Put more clearly, this is *one* of many things that the Holy Spirit does in the life of the follower of Jesus—the Holy Spirit is not to be compartmentalized or marginalized to certain expressive denominations or to the confines of a building on Sunday mornings. No, my friends. The Holy Spirit does indeed fill the believer, but then the believer is empowered to go out and declare as we see in Acts 2:11. People from different countries who spoke different languages said, "We hear them declaring the wonders of God in our own tongues."

The crowds in the streets were amazed, and "they asked one another, 'What does this mean?'"[6] And in response, Peter—who had denied his friend and Messiah but who had just been touched and filled with the Holy Spirit—stood up with confidence. Before thousands, Peter declares that the ministry of the Holy Spirit is for young and old, men and women. The work of the Holy Spirit was promised by God so many years earlier, and now as followers of Jesus we are walking in His promised gift.[7]

If the believers in the first century needed the Holy Spirit, and if Gideon needed the Holy Spirit, and if the Holy Spirit was present in Genesis at the creation of the world, why would you try to be a spouse, a parent, a friend, or a leader without the empowerment of the Holy Spirit? Yes, God has beautiful plans for your life. Yes, He wants to use your life for His glory. Yes, He wants to shine so brightly through you. All of that is true, but He is not asking you to do these things separated from who He is and the power that is supplied through the Holy Spirit.

THE HOLY SPIRIT GOES BEFORE YOU

First Corinthians 12:3 says, "Therefore I want you to know that no one who is speaking by the Spirit of God says, 'Jesus be cursed,' and no one can say, 'Jesus is Lord,' except by the Holy Spirit." This verse teaches us that you can't even be drawn to God, you can't even find the gift of salvation in Jesus, unless the Holy Spirit is the one who empowers you to say "Jesus is Lord" in the first place.

So let me make this clear: Your desire to read the Bible, your hunger for the things of God, your longing to walk more closely with Him, even your willingness to read a book like this, have been orchestrated by God because the Holy Spirit goes before you. It's called *prevenient grace*, which, simply put, means that before any man or woman seeks God, God first seeks that man or woman.

You and I are beneficiaries of the work of the Holy Spirit—His moving on our hearts, convicting us of sin, opening our eyes to the beauty and wonder of who Jesus is, drawing us to the forgiveness, salvation, and mercy that is found in the death, burial, and resurrection of Jesus proclaimed in His gospel. You and I are by-products of the Holy Spirit hovering over the earth and saying to every man, woman, boy, and girl in every language and in every culture, "You are only saved by faith in Jesus." And once you responded to the work of the Holy Spirit, Ephesians 1:13 tells us, "you also were included in Christ when you heard the message of truth, the gospel of your salvation. When you believed, you were marked in him with a seal, the promised Holy Spirit."

Your hunger for the things of God, your longing to walk more closely with Him, even your willingness to read a book like this, have been orchestrated by God because the Holy Spirit goes before you.

You are drawn to God by the Holy Spirit. You can't be saved without the Holy Spirit. You are sealed with the Holy Spirit. You are then filled with the Holy Spirit so you can be the hands and feet of God to accomplish what He has called you to do.

Please pause right now. Maybe you need to ask God for forgiveness because you've been trying to live a life for Him separated from the power that's provided by Him in the Holy Spirit. Perhaps you need to tear down the false altar of believing your good works are enough to accomplish what God is calling you to do. Perhaps you need to ask the Holy Spirit to open your eyes to who He really is so you can see the wonder and the beauty of His work all throughout the Holy Scriptures and see that same work done in your life. I'll tell you this: We need more Gideons in our day.

We need more people who are willing to pray, "Holy Spirit, fill me, but then move me out of my comfort zone in this room that I'm in, and bring me into the streets so the people can hear the wonders of God declared in a language that they understand."

I don't know all the thoughts or questions or worries you have right now, but I pray that the Holy Spirit is stirring in your heart so that you would open yourself up to His work and partner with God to accomplish His kingdom coming and His will being done on earth as it is in heaven.[8]

Before Gideon wins this next epic battle, the Holy Spirit comes upon him. And before your next epic battle, I would implore you and encourage you to pause and begin to see not just God the Father and God the Son but God the Holy Spirit, the one Jesus promised would come and walk with us. He will remind us of the Word and will keep us in alignment with it. All these verses we've read, and so many more we haven't, are proof of the importance and essentialness of the Holy Spirit. Allow these words from the Holy Bible to renew your mind and raise your awareness of the work the Spirit is already doing in your life.

Some of us have incredible physical experiences when the Holy Spirit shows His power, while others don't. You may not shed any tears, you may feel zero goosebumps, but all of us need to pause and say, "Holy Spirit, You already sealed me and filled me up until I overflow. And I live a life of love and surrender that points everyone I know and everyone I don't know to Jesus."

This is your mission, should you choose to accept it. This is your challenge, my friend. Take the step. Yield your heart. Let the Word of God cleanse and renew your mind, and then walk forward into the plans and purposes God has for you with confidence, conviction, and humility. Because the Holy Spirit's work isn't designed to keep you hiding like we originally saw in the life of Gideon. The Holy Spirit is going to empower you to move! The time is now. This is your push. Pop the clutch. Let's drive into the call God has for you to love Him and serve your world.

7

NOT ENOUGH IS ALL YOU NEED

I am very good with directions. Some people are direction-ally challenged, while I am directionally gifted. I think I got it from my awesome mom. It may be a strange flex to talk about my elite ability to navigate from point A to point B, but we all need to celebrate our various skills. With that being said, I like to be extra sure I know where I'm going, so I still use a map app and watch every turn and every stoplight as I listen to Siri directing me. And yet I still sometimes feel a little unsure. Again, I'm not a person who gets lost easily. I have all this technology at my fingertips, my hearing is good, my sight is good, but I still find myself questioning whether I'm going to find the right location.

I'm assuming you have to be a little bit like this. You know how we're looking for a particular address and we turn down the music? It's not like the music was impeding our sight, but I guess it was hindering our concentration.

We don't want to miss the place we're trying to get to. We don't even like being late. All of us wanna end up at the right location, on time, dressed appropriately, ready for the moment.

Here was Gideon, directions in hand, if you will. An angel of the Lord had spoken to him. A food offering had been miraculously consumed by fire.[1] The Lord had spoken to him and declared He is peace. And Gideon had been empowered and touched by the Holy Spirit.

He knew who the enemy was, he knew where the enemy was, and he had summoned leaders from all throughout the land to stand with him as he accomplished the task God had set before him. And with all that, he still stepped to the side of the stage and whispered to God, "Hey, can You do me a favor? I'm going to put this shirt down on the ground, and I'd like for You to make this sign for me." And God in His grace did it. Then Gideon had the audacity to ask the Lord to reverse the miracle. Was Gideon trying to get out of his calling? Was he trying to sabotage what God had put in front of him? Or was he just really overwhelmed and scared? We'll have to ask Gideon when we get to heaven—it could be all of the above. But what I know for all of us is, even if we have the clearest directions in the world, we can still be a little unsure.

My wife and I have been married for more than twenty-five years. Oneka's my best friend. She's beautiful, articulate, fun, funny, strong, and a million other attributes I could list out. She loves Jesus with all her heart. She is a fantastic wife, a wonderful mother, and an exceptional leader. She is gifted and talented in myriad ways.

Oneka was wonderful in college too. She was fun and life-giving, a leader on our campus. All our friends were trying to connect us almost from the moment Oneka got on campus. Her friends would say things to her like, "You are the female version of Earl," which I think is a compliment, but for the record, Oneka is better than me in almost everything except basketball. If it came to a game of one-on-one, I would dominate her. Just letting that be known.

But even with Oneka being the full package on the inside and out, I was still unsure. I had prayed for my wife. I looked forward to the day I would be a husband and a father. She had everything a guy could ever ask for. And I was sitting over there like Boo Boo the Fool, wondering if I should even ask her out.

I'm not trying to paint a picture that she's perfect. No one is perfect except Jesus Christ. But Oneka is as close to perfect as I can imagine. She would give anyone the coat off her back, and I've seen her do it. She has incredible attention and care for every person in her life, and she goes above and beyond the call of duty to serve those around her.

Yet there I was sitting on the sidelines, unsure if I should ask her out. All the signs were there. The GPS blue line was clear. Siri was talking. But I didn't know if I was at the correct destination or if I should take a left. Even after we started dating, I almost broke up with Oneka twice. Not because she wasn't great, but because I was looking for an angel to come into my room and make it clear that she was supposed to be my wife. I'm not even kidding. My youth pastor had told me an angel had shown up in his room and told him to marry his wife, so that was my unrealistic standard of confirmation.

But Gideon teaches me that even if an angel or the Lord Jesus Himself came into the room and told me what I was supposed to do, it's still possible I would be uncertain and second-guess myself and what I heard. So I'm not mad at Gideon. I get it, and you do too. I like that this man's story is in the Bible. It gives me hope—if he could be as cautious and uncertain as he was and still be used by God to the level of influence and impact displayed in the Scriptures, then there is hope for all of us.

We get the chance to walk with confidence and strength because this man, Gideon, received all the insight he could possibly need and still asked God to manipulate the elements so he could have one more stable rock on which to stand. It's also beautiful that Gideon is mentioned in Hebrews alongside several faith heroes who "through faith conquered kingdoms, administered justice, and gained what was promised; who shut the mouths of lions, quenched the fury of the flames, and escaped the edge of the sword; whose weakness was turned to strength; and who became powerful in battle and routed foreign armies."[2]

This was Gideon's story: His weakness was turned into strength, and he became powerful in battle and routed foreign armies. But before he ever routed an army, he essentially asked God to do magic tricks with a fleece. This, my friends, is your man of faith. You didn't even know you were emulating Gideon when you were vacillating in the valley of indecision. You just thought there was something wrong with you. But there's nothing wrong with you. We may have the directions in hand, but when it comes time to make that final decision, we often want one more act of reassurance.

It's incredibly amazing to me that God actually obliged Gideon. If I were God, I would have pushed back on Gideon and told him to shut his mouth—I already sent an angel of the Lord. But that's not what God did. What He did was meet Gideon where he was. And as God met Gideon where he was, He pulled Gideon along into the purpose and the potential and the future that He had for him.

Let's look at the text again. Gideon said to God, "I will place a wool fleece on the threshing floor. If there is dew only on the fleece and all the ground is dry, then I will know that you will save Israel by my hand, as you said."[3]

Were all the other signs and wonders not enough? Were all the other signs from God just a waste of His time? Surely the Lord knew who He was dealing with before He ever came to Gideon. God was calling on someone I would say was a complicated human being. God was asking this man to lead a mighty army to thwart the Israelites' enemies, end oppression, and reestablish the kingdom, rule, and reign of the one true God. And our friend was over there wrestling with whether or not the ground was dry or the fleece was dry. You have got to be kidding me.

Judges 6:39 reads, "Gideon said to God, 'Do not be angry with me. Let me make just one more request.'" But honestly, friends, this is me and this is you. How many times have we asked God for just one more request? Maybe we're not getting another opportunity to test God, because He's already given us confirmation. He has given us enough of the same answer.

I never saw an angel. The only sign I had from God about my wife was peace to take another step. And I had some tremendous mentors who gave me counsel to stay in the relationship with my soon-to-be bride because my insecurity was connected to my attention being wrapped up in a girl when I wanted all my attention to be wrapped up in God.

Thank You, Jesus, for those mentors in my life. Thank You, Jesus, that I had people who would talk some sense into me. Thank You, Jesus, that I had leaders I had submitted myself to, who genuinely cared for the Lord and for me, and who helped me along the path. I did not abort the mission, but I stayed on task with my beautiful soon-to-be bride.

Let's just be honest about the uncertainty of the path. Sometimes God speaks really clearly, and we are still unsure, just like when we have the directions in our hands but still roll up to the front of the house as if we may be in the wrong place.

We might assume this was the last time Gideon asked God to confirm what He had spoken. I'd love to tell you that Gideon needed no other assurances and was filled with faith from the top of his head to the soles of his feet and was void of every ounce of fear or trepidation. But that would be a lie.

Just a little later, in Judges 7:2–3, we find that "the LORD said to Gideon, 'You have too many men. I cannot deliver Midian into their hands, or Israel would boast against me, "My own strength has saved me." Now announce to the army, "Anyone who trembles with fear may turn back and leave Mount Gilead." ' So twenty-two thousand men left, while ten thousand remained."

Oh snap. Can you believe this? The army has dropped to a third of its original number. I'm no war strategist, but it seems pretty clear to me that when going to war, you want the largest force possible to overwhelm your enemy and win the battle quickly.

But God, in His infinite wisdom, decided to minimize Gideon's army. I'm guessing Gideon had been thinking there weren't *enough* men, yet God said there were too many, so Gideon followed the leading of the Lord.

In verse four, God told Gideon, "There are still too many men. Take them down to the water, and I will thin them out for you there." And if Gideon was remotely like me, I can hear him muttering something like, "Oh no, thank You, Lord. You don't have to do that for me. I'm happy and content with the ten thousand that I have, since You already sent twenty-two thousand away. Lord, let's not thin anything out. Let's keep everything as thick as we possibly can have it. We don't need any receding hairline here, Lord. Go ahead and turn this into a full-fledged Afro. No comb-over necessary."

But Judges 7:5–7 shows Gideon following God's instructions:

> The Lord told him, "Separate those who lap the water with their tongues as a dog laps from those who kneel down to drink." Three hundred of them drank from cupped hands, lapping like

dogs. All the rest got down on their knees to drink.

The LORD said to Gideon, "With the three hundred men that lapped I will save you and give the Midianites into your hands. Let all the others go home."

To be clear, Gideon started with thirty-two thousand men, and now his army had been reduced by 99 percent to a tiny group of three hundred men.

I don't know about you, but it seems to me that losing nearly all your resources wouldn't instill a ton of confidence about facing a task that already felt insurmountable. Does this feel familiar? Maybe we say, "Wow, Lord. Thank You. But this is a humble, sarcastic 'thank You' because I don't really feel thankful. I feel scared and upset, and even that abandoned feeling is coming back."

Because, to be clear, you can be called by God and empowered by the Spirit of God and still be a little bit unsure and a lot bit upset. If that's the space you find yourself in, again, you're not alone. This just happens to be the moment you're in, but these moments will not last forever.

God had made Gideon's army smaller and smaller and smaller, but not without reason. With just three hundred men, no one could boast in their own powers or strength or military strategy. Everyone would understand that it was by the grace and power of God that they were released from their oppressors. Can't you just see Gideon sitting around looking at three hundred people, thinking, *I don't think this is gonna work*? And you probably wouldn't think it would work either. And I know that because most of us have had a dream, looked at what we had in hand to accomplish said dream, and concluded we didn't have enough. That may be one of the primary reasons you're reading this book— because you keep being frustrated with lack. But the reason you don't have enough is because God has given you exactly what you need so that He can get the glory when the task is accomplished. Not enough is all you need.

Not enough is all you need.

Of course, you have to seek wisdom. Of course, you have to set things up as best as you possibly can. Of course, strategy and common sense are good, and having the right team around you is essential. All of that is 100 percent true. But what is also true is sometimes God will give you less than you think is necessary so that you don't lean on yourself but on Him for His strength and provision. "Trust in the LORD with all your heart and lean not on your own understanding; in all your ways submit to him, and he will make your paths straight."[4]

Without a doubt, there's a principle here in the story of Gideon that it's not necessarily having a lot of people around you that's good. It's more important to have the right people around you. Remember the first twenty-two thousand who left? They left because they were trembling with fear. That's what Judges 7:3 tells us: "Now announce to the army, 'Anyone who trembles with fear may turn back and leave Mount Gilead.' So twenty-two thousand men left." Gideon had an army of thirty-two thousand, but more than two-thirds of the soldiers in that army were ravaged with fear and trembling internally. What would that have been like for the three hundred who ended up staying with Gideon? What if they had been surrounded by twenty-two thousand people who were fearful and anxious? How do we think that would have worked out for Gideon and the three hundred?

Yes, there are times when a small group changes the culture and the tone of the multitude. Certainly that can happen. But there are also other times when it's a waste of energy to try to convince twenty-two thousand people of something that three hundred people are already convinced of. I would rather have three hundred fully convinced people than 22,300 people who are unconvinced.

Who are the people you have in your life right now? Who are the greatest influences? Who's talking to you, giving you insight and clarity about who you are or where God is trying to take you? You may have heard the old adage "Show me your friends and I'll show you your future." Some of us have been content having a large group of friends around us, when really we need just a few who will push us forward. Perhaps as you shed who you used to be, God is going to ask you to transition and be willing to release some friends in your life.

The cool thing for Gideon is this is not the first time he

had to tear down or cut. He did that when he snuck onto his father's land and cut down the Asherah pole and destroyed the altar to Baal. And maybe as you deal with some things in your past, it'll give you confidence to deal with your present, to assess those around you and say, with humility and confidence, "God, who is not supposed to be with me?"

Because there are some friends who cannot go with you into your next battle. They will spread too much poison, too many lies, and they will distort the hope and the lives of those who are ready to move forward.

I've been on a lot of teams throughout the years, and there is nothing like a negative attitude to suck the life out of a team that's trying to accomplish a task. Negative people are toxic. They're draining, and they're complicated. A lot of times they don't listen to hope, because they're too busy listening to fear. I've got some great friends in my life. They're not perfect, but they're great friends. The people who are closest to me—they're life-giving. And when I'm a friend to someone, I try to be life-giving as well. I try to speak words of encouragement and hope. Without a doubt, I will challenge my friends, but I don't challenge in a way to tear them down. I challenge to build them up because I recognize that if someone has the right people around them, then it makes it all the sweeter and better when God accomplishes what He's wanting to accomplish through them.

Show me your friends and I'll show you your future. This works for married couples and single people. This works whether you're older or younger. If you get around a bunch of people who believe it can't be done, don't be surprised when you begin to believe it can't be done either.

But it's a game changer when you get around people who have a mountain-moving kind of faith, who believe God is "able to do immeasurably more than all we ask or imagine,"[5] who understand that God created the world and everything in it just by speaking life. These people who speak words of life are sowing seeds of greatness into our souls, and we do the same when we speak words of life into them.

This creates a massive rotation of momentum, and this centripetal force doesn't make you sick. It inspires you to want to ask God for the impossible. This type of environment and these types of friends encourage you to pray bold prayers. These kinds of people are the ones who see you struggling, but they know you still have more inside of you and will be present to give you a helping hand or an encouraging word. These are the people who will pray for you when you are sick, who will sit by your bedside and ask God to work in your life when you feel like you have given everything you could and you want to throw in the towel. Not only do I want to be surrounded by these people, but I wanna be this kind of person. I wanna be this type of friend. A life-giving, life-transforming agent. An ambassador of heaven on earth. I want to be this kind of person: When people get around me, they start believing all things are possible.

Are you willing to cut away? Are you willing to be misunderstood? Are you willing to be talked about behind your back at times, or maybe left out and skipped over? Sometimes you gotta cut away twenty-two thousand so that you're surrounded by the right people.

Sometimes you gotta cut away twenty-two
thousand so that you're surrounded by the
right people.

From the end of Judges 6 all the way into chapter 7, we
still see Gideon battling with fear. I want you to understand
that you may never graduate from some struggles. They
might always be closer than you want them to be. But sometimes the struggle is the thing that keeps us humble. It
helps us see ourselves rightly as we see ourselves surrendered and dependent upon almighty God.

In 2 Corinthians 12:8–10, Paul prays about a particu-
larly stubborn challenge he's struggling with:

> Three times I pleaded with the Lord to take it
> away from me. But he said to me, "My grace is
> sufficient for you, for my power is made perfect in
> weakness." Therefore I will boast all the more
> gladly about my weaknesses, so that Christ's
> power may rest on me. That is why, for Christ's
> sake, I delight in weaknesses, in insults, in hard-
> ships, in persecutions, in difficulties. For when I
> am weak, then I am strong.

I know that's a little countercultural, and I know that's
different from the wisdom of the day, but I'm going with
Scripture rather than society. I boast in my weaknesses so
that Christ's power can rest on me. Sometimes it's good to
say "I'm scared." I'm scared, but I'm not quitting. I'm scared,

but I'm not throwing in the towel. I'm scared, but I'm not going to sit on the side of the road and sulk. I'm scared, but I will not forfeit what God has called me to do, because I recognize it's not about me; it's about Him and about Him reaching others through me. I'm scared, but I will stay at my post. I'm scared, but I will keep moving forward. I will continue to trust God in the middle of crying huge tears. I'm scared, but I will not turn away from what God has asked me to turn toward. I'm scared, but I'm still going to trust that God knows what He is doing. And even when I don't know all that He knows, I can trust that He knows better than me.

As we continue on this journey, we are about to see a massive change happen on the inside of Gideon. We are about to see a switch. We are about to see a change in language and even a change in posture. And as we see this in Gideon, I'm praying that God and our friends would see this change in us too.

8

WORDS OF POWER

Words are incredibly powerful. Words matter.

When our oldest son was five years old, maybe six, I was putting him to bed one night, as I have loved to do from the time my kids were little until the age when they'll no longer let me do it.

On this particular night, he started scratching at his hand and saying something, but his words to me were incredibly hard to hear. I asked him, "Why are you scratching the back of your hand?"

"Dad, I'm trying to scratch off my skin so it can be white."

I was floored. Why would my amazing, handsome, strong, young, brown-skinned son want his skin to be a different color? And in his innocence, he talked about a lot of the friends he had around him, friends in his wonderful private school who didn't look like him, and they all had peach skin. Obviously, this was hard to hear. It was difficult to digest because we love how God made him. We know that God put him in the skin he is in on purpose and for a purpose, and we also know that there is no skin color that's greater than any other skin color.

But here was our five-year-old, trying to scratch off his skin. I've only shared this story a couple of times—it's still hard to even bring it to mind. I talked to my wife that night and said, "We've gotta do something here." So we started something that we call Words of Power. Now, at our bedtime routine with all our kids, we begin by sharing some scriptures. The first scripture we share is Psalm 136:1–9. Oneka or I say the first half of each verse, beginning with verse 1: "Give thanks to the LORD, for he is good." And then whichever child we are with says the unchanging second half of each verse: "His love endures forever."

Then we say the Shoreline City creed, which we also say every weekend at all locations of our church.

> I am loved by God. I cannot earn it. I cannot lose
> it. In Christ, I am forgiven and made brand-new.
> I live with passion and purpose. I am empowered
> by the Spirit to be the church in the world and to
> live for the glory of God.

Next, we quote Daniel 1:4 and personalize it: I am a young man [or woman] "without any physical defect, handsome, showing aptitude for every kind of learning, well informed, quick to understand, and qualified to serve in the king's palace."

And for the last portion of the Words of Power, we contextualize positive declarations for whatever season our kids are in. For example: I'm blessed, I'm healed, and I'm full of faith. I love Jesus. I love my church. I'm filled with hope. I'm filled with life. I'm filled with purpose. I'm honest and thankful. I'm courageous. I love how God made me. I love my skin. I will be one of the greatest people of God in my generation. I'm here to serve, called to lead and to live for the glory of God.

The Words of Power were a direct assault against the insecurity and lies that the devil was trying to insert into the heart of our son. We spoke these words over our son, and each and every night, he would repeat the Words of Power. I'm happy to tell you all these years later, he is not scratching at his skin but is walking into rooms with all the confidence that we would want him to have, because he knows who God has called and made him to be.

I'm sure a lot of things influenced that confidence, but I'm also convinced that the Words of Power that we speak every night—words birthed from the Scriptures—have helped to change and transform his heart and his mind and how he sees himself. Words matter. I can tell a lot about you by how you speak about yourself. And in the next scene of Gideon's life, we find out that God has been setting the stage for Gideon. You can write this down and remember it for the rest of your life: Even when you're afraid, God is still setting the stage.

Let's take a look at this scene in Judges 7:13–18:

Gideon arrived just as a man was telling a friend his dream. "I had a dream," he was saying. "A round loaf of barley bread came tumbling into the Midianite camp. It struck the tent with such force that the tent overturned and collapsed."

His friend responded, "This can be nothing other than the sword of Gideon son of Joash, the Israelite. God has given the Midianites and the whole camp into his hands."

When Gideon heard the dream and its interpretation, he bowed down and worshiped. He returned to the camp of Israel and called out, "Get up! The LORD has given the Midianite camp into your hands." Dividing the three hundred men into three companies, he placed trumpets and empty jars in the hands of all of them, with torches inside.

"Watch me," he told them. "Follow my lead. When I get to the edge of the camp, do exactly as I do. When I and all who are with me blow our trumpets, then from all around the camp blow yours and shout, 'For the LORD and for Gideon.'"

God was putting Gideon's name in rooms that Gideon had yet to walk into. And I pray that God is doing the same thing in your life, that He is putting your name in rooms and that you are going to be a person of influence for His glory. God has your name in rooms where you have yet to set your feet so that His kingdom can be expanded.

Then Gideon's words began to change. He said things

like, "Get up," "Watch me," "Follow my lead." But you remember what he was saying in the beginning, don't you? When the Lord called him a mighty warrior, Gideon's response was, "Pardon me, my lord, . . . but how can I save Israel? My clan is the weakest in Manasseh, and I am the least in my family."[1] These words were the outflow of Gideon's self-talk.

But we haven't yet addressed Manasseh. Why would Gideon think being a small clan in Manasseh was a legitimate excuse? Well, Genesis 41 has answers for us.

You're likely familiar with Joseph: This man had dreams, and his brothers weren't excited about his dreams, so his brothers betrayed him and sold him into slavery. After all this betrayal, Joseph found himself in prison. But in a stunning reversal, because he had a knack for interpreting God's messages in dreams, he became the second-in-command over all of Egypt. God gave him a place of prominence and influence in a powerful nation.

While Joseph was in Egypt, he had two sons. "Joseph named his firstborn Manasseh and said, 'It is because God has made me forget all my trouble and all my father's household.' The second son he named Ephraim and said, 'It is because God has made me fruitful in the land of my suffering.'"[2]

In the midst of all the pain and suffering and difficulty he had to navigate, Joseph was blessed with these amazing sons and gave them names to remind himself and everyone else how God had been faithful and carried him through the hardest season of his life.

In a powerful moment of redemption, Joseph met his

brothers again, forgave them, and reunited with his father. After a few years, his father, Jacob, was old and nearing his death. His strength was waning, and Joseph took his sons to say goodbye and receive their grandfather's blessing.

Joseph presented his sons to his father, Jacob, who was called Israel then, but a switch took place. In that culture, older siblings were supposed to receive the greater blessing. Notice the details here. "Joseph took both of them, Ephraim on his right toward Israel's left hand and Manasseh on his left toward Israel's right hand, and brought them close to him. But Israel reached out his right hand and put it on Ephraim's head, though he was the younger, and crossing his arms, he put his left hand on Manasseh's head, even though Manasseh was the firstborn."[3] When Joseph saw his father crossing his arms, he tried to correct him, but Jacob explained the switch was intentional. "So he put Ephraim ahead of Manasseh."[4]

Now, if you're Ephraim in this story, you're probably pumped. You're thrilled. And, friends, this can even be incredibly encouraging for those of us who are like Ephraim, because sometimes we are given a blessing we never thought possible. Oh man, perhaps Ephraim was doing the Cupid Shuffle at this moment. Ephraim had received the firstborn's blessing. Grandpa crossed his arms, and the blessing cannot be reversed. The words have been spoken.

But if you're Manasseh, if you're the firstborn and Grandpa's right hand was headed toward you but then moved and rested on your little brother, think about the confusion and the hurt you might feel. Manasseh saw his father, Joseph, trying to fix it, but Grandpa would not allow it. Put yourself in Manasseh's sandals. What thoughts might have been going through his head? *I must not be good enough. I must not be strong enough. I must not have the gifts and talents and abilities that are needed to carry a firstborn blessing. What's wrong with me? Why don't I measure up? Yes, I'm glad I got a blessing from my grandfather, but it's not the blessing that I wanted, and it's not even the blessing that was set aside for me.*

The reason I think it's clear that Manasseh was disappointed that he didn't receive the greater blessing is because we can see in his family line a mentality of "least and weakest" all the way to Gideon.

The time between Manasseh and Gideon wasn't five years. It wasn't fifty years. It was well over five hundred years. *Five hundred years.* It seems that moment when the arms crossed was still stuck in the mindset and the heart of the descendants of Manasseh. Now God was trying to talk to one of Manasseh's descendants, and the underlying narrative of "not good enough" from hundreds of years before was once again raising its ugly head.

"Pardon me, my lord," Gideon said in Judges 6:15, "but how can I save Israel? My clan is the weakest in Manasseh." Gideon was implying, "Lord, You know what happens to those of us in the line of Manasseh. We don't measure up. We get passed over. We're not leaders. We get the leftovers. You obviously have the wrong person."

Words matter. What you speak over yourself matters. So you must ask yourself the question, Is what you're speaking over yourself consistent with what God says about you?

> What you speak over yourself matters. So you must ask yourself the question, Is what you're speaking over yourself consistent with what God says about you?

So here is Gideon, rehearsing the negative narrative that had haunted his family line for hundreds of years. Like a virus, it had spread from generation to generation. But God speaks a better word. God knew the plan and the purpose and the call that He'd put in Gideon. He knew how He wanted to use Gideon's life for His glory, but the words of the years had gotten in the way.

The night before Gideon was to lead his army into battle against the Midianites, he was still afraid—still convinced he was the least and weakest. God told him, "If you are afraid to attack, go down to the camp with your servant Purah and listen to what they are saying." Gideon snuck into the camp where their enemies had settled as "thick as locusts."[5]

Travel back with me outside the enemy's tent as Gideon overheard a dream that was about to ignite his destiny. "Gideon arrived just as a man was telling a friend his dream. 'I had a dream,' he was saying. 'A round loaf of barley bread came tumbling into the Midianite camp. It struck the tent with such force that the tent overturned and collapsed.' His friend responded, 'This can be nothing other than the sword of Gideon son of Joash, the Israelite. God has given the Midianites and the whole camp into his hands.'"[6]

When Gideon heard how God had equipped and pre-pared him for victory, he did not immediately run to the battle. Instead, he dropped to his knees. He bowed down and worshipped.[7] Do not skip over this. On the verge of crossing into the plan and the purpose that God has for you, do not skip worship. As you dream about your future and your fulfilling the plans and purposes God has for your life, do not skip worship.

In that place of surrender and worship, Gideon's heart was being molded and his mind was being renewed to understand who God is and what God is able to do. It was in bowing down and worshipping that Gideon was coming into new life, because the word of God had been chasing him down, and God had been declaring His truth over him, and finally it seems the penny had dropped. Gideon saw what God was doing the clearest he'd seen it in all the time that he'd been interacting with the Lord. He'd torn down his altars, gathered an army, and watched that army be cut down to 1 percent. He'd obeyed the Lord and taken steps even when he was afraid. Now finally, he saw God's goodness.

With Gideon we can say, "God, You are good. You are worthy. God, there is no one like You. You are holy and above all. You are the ruler of the earth, the sustainer of all things, the beginning and the end. God, You are everything, and I bow my mind, my will, my emotions, my fears, my brokenness, my *life* to You. I worship You, and I serve You, because I'm not just serving my purpose—I'm serving You who have given me my purpose. So I will not idolize my pain, I will not idolize my brokenness, I will not idolize my insecurity, and I am done disqualifying myself from the positions You have called me to."

Maybe you need to pause right now and bow down in worship, and don't just bow down and talk to God about your brokenness. Bow down and talk to God about His awesomeness. And just in case you're still not sure about your own qualifications, read Colossians 1:12: "[God] has qualified you to share in the inheritance of his holy people in the kingdom of light."

Words have power. Posture matters. And we see a switch and a change in the words of Gideon.

When Gideon got up from kneeling and worshipping, he had a new sense of confidence and conviction. Judges 7:15 says, "He returned to the camp of Israel and called out, 'Get up! The LORD has given the Midianite camp into your hands.'" This was a massive departure from the insecurity and fear. Now Gideon was speaking with authority and leadership: "The Lord *has* given the Midianites into your hands." Not "The Lord *might* give the enemy into our hands." No, God had already done it. It was a done deal. Gideon knew now that God had gone before them. He had already prepared the way, because this was about Him and not about them.

Get up, get up, get up.

I pray this over you, too, that you'll feel the urgency to get up. As you say yes to what God is calling you to do, you will then inspire others to say yes to what God is calling them to do.

Get up. The Lord has prepared the way.

It gets better. In Judges 7:17, Gideon told his men, "Watch me. . . . Follow my lead." Wow. Are you serious? God did a work in his heart, and the work in his heart was now changing the words of his mouth. May that be true for all of us. May the work of the Holy Spirit in our lives affect us so much that it seeps into how we post on social media, how we talk to our family and our friends, how we lead our co-workers, how we run our businesses, how we move forward in the purpose that God has for our lives. May our lives say, Watch me and follow my lead.

Some of us wanna just jump to "Watch me. . . . Follow my lead," but you have yet to be the type of leader who bows down and worships. For those who are followers of Jesus, we don't lead by lording over people; we lead by serving people. But let us first bow down and worship and understand what it means to serve the Lord.

The authority with which Gideon was able to lead was directly connected to the humility with which he was willing to serve. His language has changed: "Watch me. . . . Follow my lead." Wow. Wow. Words matter. Proverbs 18:21 reads, "The tongue has the power of life and death, and those who love it will eat its fruit."

In the same way that "I'm ugly," "I can't do it," "I don't matter," "It's too hard" can shape the narrative and the reality of your future, so can "I've been called by God. I'm qualified because of the finished work of Jesus Christ. I've been put here to live for the glory of God. I was born for such a time as this, and I will make a difference in my generation for His fame and His glory."

It is possible for you to go from scratching your skin to

leading like a champion. It is possible for you to step fully into who God has called you to be.

Words matter.

Your name may be in rooms you're not in yet, like we saw with Gideon. And it's beautiful to see the favor of God and how He's able to lead and guide your life and put you in the right place at the right time with the right people. But if the words you speak over yourself are inconsistent with the Scripture that God has given to govern your life, you can unintentionally put a kink in the hose as God is trying to flow the water of the river of life through your existence.

Words have power.

We will probably not get this correct right away. Look at the journey Gideon had to go through. I mean, God showed up under an oak, and Gideon had to be honest with Him. Then Gideon had to navigate the presence, power, favor, and peace, and he had to obey God by tearing down his father's altars. He needed to be empowered by the Spirit and get the right people around him. He had to go through quite a journey. This was not a straight line. It was a little bit like the line of Joseph's life that went up and down, left and right, curving around and putting him in a spot he didn't want to be in. Then somehow, some way, by God's sovereign hand of grace, he ended up where he was supposed to be. Can you relate?

It's a roller coaster at times, so please don't try to make this a linear path. This, my friends, is a winding journey. It's life, and we live it surrendered to God. Put another way, "I have been crucified with Christ and I no longer live, but Christ lives in me. The life I now live in the body, I live by faith in the Son of God, who loved me and gave himself for me."[8] This requires faith.

> Echo what God's Word says about your life, because when your words change, your life can change.

If you are going to be the young person, the older person, the man, the woman, the leader that God has called you to be, you do not get to graduate from faith, from trusting in God and in what He has said. I pray that you would begin to echo what God's Word says about your life, because when your words change, your life can change.

I encourage you to sit down and write your own Words of Power. May they flow right from Scripture. Repeat these truths over yourself every night and every morning. And as you understand who you are in Christ and what God has spoken over your life, begin to declare these words while you are on your way to work or as you're working out. In times when you are feeling incredibly worthless, speak what God says about you, not the negative narrative you've been repeating for years. Because, my friend, you were born for such a time as this. And it's time for you to say yes to all God has said about you and what He's called you to do.

9
THE SWITCH AND THE CHASE

On October 30, 1974, one of the greatest sporting events of the twentieth century took place—the Rumble in the Jungle, a boxing match between heavyweight champion George Foreman and Muhammad Ali. Foreman was twenty-five years old and undefeated. Ali was thirty-two, and few people believed he had a chance of winning the fight. As a matter of fact, Ali was the underdog, with four-to-one odds. Foreman was young and strong, and he could hit like a tank. The fight was held in what is now the Democratic Republic of the Congo, with sixty thousand spectators and as many as one billion people watching on television worldwide.[1]

From the very first round, Foreman was dominating the fight—absolutely dominating. Ali was throwing some punches, but he was on the ropes much of the time, being pounded with lefts and rights from Foreman. But in the eighth round, things changed. Ali turned the tide of this boxing match and went from a defensive position to an incredibly strong offensive position.[2]

Muhammad Ali used a new technique that is now called the rope-a-dope—he allowed his opponent to tire himself out by throwing punch after punch after punch while Ali sat in a defensive posture, waiting for the right moment to pounce. The right moment came, and the fight changed drastically. Ali went from absorbing all of Foreman's blows to knocking out the undisputed and undefeated heavyweight champion of the world. Put another way, he went from the defensive to the offensive, and this is what we see in our man Gideon.

> Dividing the three hundred men into three companies, [Gideon] placed trumpets and empty jars in the hands of all of them, with torches inside.
>
> "Watch me," he told them. "Follow my lead. When I get to the edge of the [Midianite] camp, do exactly as I do. When I and all who are with me blow our trumpets, then from all around the camp blow yours and shout, 'For the LORD and for Gideon.'"
>
> Gideon and the hundred men with him reached the edge of the camp. . . . The three companies blew the trumpets and smashed the jars. . . .

> When the three hundred trumpets sounded,
> the LORD caused the men throughout the
> camp to turn on each other with their swords.
> (Judges 7:16–20, 22)

The enemy army turned on each other and fled, and the Israelites routed them out of that valley. Gideon sent messengers throughout Ephraim, calling the nation of Israel to come down and join the force to push the Midianites out of the land.[3]

Gideon went from playing defense—from speaking words of insecurity and fear and doubt—to rallying the troops, calling in people from the surrounding areas, and doing something we had not yet seen him do. He pursued the Midianites.[4]

For years, the children of Israel had been on the ropes with the Midianites. For years, they'd been taking hits. For years, their land and their crops and their livestock had been ravaged. The Midianite army, too numerous to count, had covered the land. Remember Judges 6:6 told us that "Midian so impoverished the Israelites that they cried out to the LORD for help."

The Midianites had been the undisputed heavyweight champions for years, and Israel—God's chosen people— had been on the ropes. Yes, Israel was living in bondage because of their sin. They had turned away from God. But they were on the ropes, nonetheless. They had been getting hit left and right, left and right, body shots, head shots— just covering up, hoping to make it to another round.

That's how many of us have lived our lives. Taking hit

after hit, just covering up, hoping to make it another day. Unfortunately, there are so many marriages like that, so many business leaders with this mindset, so many students and teenagers just taking the hits, thinking there's nothing else they can do. Maybe you're seeing problems in society or the scarcity of food, and you've just been taking the blows. Or you thought the evils of sex trafficking and the poison of pornography were unstoppable, so you counted yourself out from doing anything to make a difference. Maybe you've seen your family line go down the same broken path over and over, generation after generation, and you've simply accepted that it is what it is. But you are reading these words now, you see Gideon rising up and playing offense, and you know it's time to stop absorbing the blows and begin to punch back.

Gideon, after all he had been through—after bowing down and worshipping, after changing his mouth to be in alignment with God's word, and after winning a tremendous battle—went from being on the ropes and being hit to now being the one throwing the lefts and rights, the haymakers, the uppercuts, and the body shots. He's saying, "It's time to go on the offensive."

It's time for us to switch to the offensive. It's time for you to move beyond just absorbing hits and begin giving the hits. You might ask, "Who are we hitting?"

That's the question of the hour. The assignment will be different for each of us. God has prepared us to be mighty warriors for specific battles. Some of us will wage war on demonic mindsets, the brokenness and dysfunction of our world, or the systems that are keeping people hurt, marginalized, and forgotten. Or we might take the initiative to pray in our homes rather than just letting the culture of our house exist without any intentionality. For others, we'll look at foster care and figure out how to insert the kingdom of God and scriptural principles into a system that was set up to help families but on so many occasions wears out the workers and creates heartache and pain.

Going on the offensive will look different for each of us, but it will share the same attitude, the same spirit. The spirit that says, "I'm not going down." The spirit that says, "I will not quit. I'm going to move forward to fight against what's been fighting me."

Maybe some thoughts, lies, shame, and guilt have kept you hiding like Gideon in a winepress threshing wheat. We're saying no, it's time to punch back at that insecurity and fear and doubt, because you've been given weapons that are mighty through God for pulling down strongholds.[5]

It's time to attack.

I almost got in a fistfight recently. My wife went to get her lashes done. Her friend was kind enough to drop her off in a little parking spot near her appointment. They had been parked for ninety seconds as my bride finished grabbing her things out of the car, when another stylist in the building started yelling at my wife and her friend. This guy was angry because they had blocked his spot. Again, they'd been in place for no more than ninety seconds. Oneka was unnerved, rightfully so. She tried to go into the building, and the guy followed and yelled at her. Oneka had to go up three flights of stairs, and this jerk was on her heels, mocking her and disrespecting her. He continued to shout at her

after she entered the door of her salon. She called me and
told me what was happening. She told me she was scared,
concerned for her safety, and I immediately dropped what I
was doing and headed over. I was mad. And I mean *mad*. As
I was driving, it hit me: I'm a pastor. I'm not allowed to
whoop somebody's behind because they disrespected my
wife. So I called the head of our security team to get some
wisdom. He used to be a police officer, and he gave me some
great advice on what to say and what not to say. He then
said he'd meet me at the salon to confront the guy. I called
another friend, and we were on our way. We found my wife,
safe and sound, and we went to the guy's door to clearly and
strongly let him know we were there to ask him to apolo-
gize. No hands were thrown. No names were called. But you
could 100 percent feel that we were not backing down. We
were there to protect my queen. We were moving on the
offensive.

Jesus gave one of His signature profound lines while travel-
ing with His disciples. He first asked His disciples who the
public thought He was, and then He asked them,

> "Who do you say I am?"
> Simon Peter answered, "You are the Messiah,
> the Son of the living God."
> Jesus replied, "Blessed are you, Simon son of
> Jonah, for this was not revealed to you by flesh

and blood, but by my Father in heaven. And I tell
you that you are Peter, and on this rock I will
build my church, and the gates of Hades will not
overcome it." (Matthew 16:15–18)

*I will build My church, and the gates of hell will not over-
come it.*

Jesus painted a picture of the church He is building, and
this church is powerful. And this church has a mission. In
Matthew 28:19–20, Jesus told those who followed Him,
"Therefore go and make disciples of all nations, baptizing
them in the name of the Father and of the Son and of the
Holy Spirit, and teaching them to obey everything I have
commanded you. And surely I am with you always, to the
very end of the age." Do you see what kind of church Jesus
is building? Do you see that His church has been given a call
and a mission to go?

Jesus declared His church will be stronger than the gates
of hell. In His day, there was an actual place near where
Jesus was walking with His disciples that people called the
gates of hell—a cave they believed was a gateway to the
underworld.[6] As Jesus stood atop this particular location in
Caesarea Philippi—maybe in plain view of the gates of
hell—He testified to the strength of His church. In a place
where people had sacrificed to false gods, where people had
been fearful of darkness, He announced that the church He
was building would not be afraid or back down.

This is the type of church Jesus is building. Maybe some
of us thought church was just supposed to be cute, sweet,

innocuous, nonconfrontational, have no fight, and have no reason to put gloves on. But please understand: We do fight. Our fight may not look like everyone else's—we're not cussing and tearing people down—but it's a fight nonetheless. And it requires massive amounts of courage and humility. Our good fight can only be inspired by the Spirit and empowered by the Spirit, because we have been called to follow in the path of our glorious Savior, who fought the ultimate battle and won. And His fight started with words initially but led to Him sacrificing His life on our behalf before rising again in victory. And His victory is now our victory. Jesus is building a church ready and strong for the fight, but "we do not wage war as the world does."[7] We have to fight like our Savior does.

Allow me to take this a step further and say that gates are not offensive weapons. Gates are defensive tools designed to keep people out. Yes, they open to let people in, but they also keep people trapped inside. And Jesus said the gates of hell will not prevail against the church. Hear this: We are not the ones sitting back and retreating. No, we are the ones moving forward, kicking down the gates of hell to release prisoners the Enemy has kept trapped for too long.

> We are not the ones sitting back and retreating. No, we are the ones moving forward, kicking down the gates of hell to release prisoners the Enemy has kept trapped for too long.

Now, when we think of church, our minds tend to run to polite people, clean buildings, and side hugs. Or maybe we think of the word *safe:* safe buildings, safe people, safe preaching, safe vision—all on the safe side of town. Safe, safe, safe. But the church Jesus is building was never designed to be safe. If you and I read through the book of Acts, we'll find that the followers of Jesus were put in some very difficult situations, and when faced with incredible obstacles, they did not run and hide but asked God for strength to move forward.

This was what Gideon was doing with the Midianites. They had kept the children of Israel locked down. And Gideon, emboldened and freed by God, moved and acted so that the Israelites would not stay in bondage and sin any longer.

The front line of the church's battle is to contend for the souls of humankind, to say, "You will not be bound forever—the gates of hell cannot stand against the power, authority, and advancement of God and His church." This is what salvation looks like. It reminds me of Jesus's last charge to His followers: "Go and make disciples of all nations, baptizing them in the name of the Father and of the Son and of the Holy Spirit."[8]

Jesus's church—which includes you and me—is not anemic and apathetic.

We can't remain stagnant any longer. It's time to move! The Holy Spirit has come, and He's called us to move in the world, to make disciples of all nations. The church that Jesus is building—you can find it kicking down the gates of hell.

✳

One of my favorite stories is found in the beginning of the book of Acts, when Peter and John, after preaching the glorious gospel, have found themselves in a heap of trouble. The religious leaders do not like the message that this Jesus, whom they killed, had risen from the dead. But that was the message nonetheless because Peter and John and a whole bunch of others witnessed that powerful resurrection, and now they were sharing it all over the known world. They'd been empowered by the Spirit, and their lives were forever changed. Acts 4:13 says that when the rulers and teachers of the law "saw the courage of Peter and John and realized that they were unschooled, ordinary men, they were astonished and they took note that these men had been with Jesus." Do you see how courage and strength were proof that Peter and John had been with Jesus? Do you see that advancement was seen as proof? Do you see that their message was centered upon the person of Christ?

They were moving forward, and their lives were being changed and transformed, but not everyone was happy about it. Whenever you step forward to be who God has called you to be, you can expect opposition, because the system that is broken in this world, the one that is governed by sin and darkness and the devil himself, is not interested in the kingdom of God being established. So as you and I move forward, we are bringing light to darkness. But just because we take some hits doesn't mean we stop moving forward. These men, they went through a lot.

They had been ridiculed and persecuted for their faith. They were beaten and imprisoned. But listen to their prayer:

> "Sovereign Lord," they said, "you made the heavens and the earth and the sea, and everything in them. You spoke by the Holy Spirit through the mouth of your servant, our father David:
>
>> "'Why do the nations rage
>>   and the peoples plot in vain?
>> The kings of the earth rise up
>>   and the rulers band together
>> against the Lord
>>   and against his anointed one.'
>
> Indeed Herod and Pontius Pilate met together with the Gentiles and the people of Israel in this city to conspire against your holy servant Jesus, whom you anointed. They did what your power and will had decided beforehand should happen. Now, Lord, consider their threats and enable your servants to speak your word with great boldness. Stretch out your hand to heal and perform signs and wonders through the name of your holy servant Jesus."
>
> After they prayed, the place where they were meeting was shaken. And they were all filled with the Holy Spirit and spoke the word of God boldly. (Acts 4:24–31)

Their prayer was not, "God, keep us safe" or "Hide us away." No, my friends, their prayer was founded in Scripture and centered on Jesus. They were filled with the Spirit, and they asked God for amazing, beautiful, and supernatural signs. Let's join them in their prayer: "God, consider those threats, but enable us to speak Your word with great boldness. Consider the difficulty, but enable Your servants to stand in strength. Consider our weaknesses, but do not let us throw in the towel, because You're not building a safe church. As a matter of fact, Your church is advancing on the doorstep of hell."

We find God's church in the proverbial enemy's territory. We find His church a little bit on the—dare I say—wild side. We find His church kicking down prison doors and announcing, "His kingdom come, His will be done on earth as it is in heaven."

This is what we begin to see in Gideon.

I don't wanna paint an easy picture. It wasn't easy for the first disciples, and it wasn't easy for Gideon. It won't be easy for us either. As a matter of fact, in Judges 8:4, we find Gideon and his men "exhausted yet keeping up the pursuit." I like that: exhausted yet keeping up the pursuit. Is that not relatable? Maybe you're exhausted by the hustle and the grind. Tired from one overwhelming world event after another. Maybe you're exhausted because your kids aren't sleeping through the night. Now, I just know there's someone reading this book whose baby started sleeping through the night at two weeks old, and the rest of us are happy for you, but also we don't like you just a little bit. Of course, that's a joke. But the reasons for our exhaustion are countless.

One night during our own season of sleepless nights, I was lying in bed next to Oneka, listening to our child cry. We didn't know why—we had already done the feeding, changed the diaper, walked, and rocked. We did everything we knew to do, and the crying would not stop. I turned to Oneka at maybe 3:17 A.M. and said, "I would rather a baby grand piano fall right on my head at this moment than deal with all these tears." Oneka and I still laugh about that moment, but we were just that exhausted.

I'm happy to say we all made it through those sleepless nights by doing what every tired parent, business leader, athlete, or student knows—you ask God for the strength, and you put one foot in front of the other. Exhausted yet keeping up the pursuit.

I fully believe that the empowerment of the Holy Spirit is going to give you some wind in your sails, but there will be times when you feel exhausted. There will be times when you feel like you can't go forward. But Gideon here reminds us that we can be tired and still continue the pursuit.

As you lean into becoming all God has called you to be, there will be times when you feel like you've given all you have to give and there's nothing left in the tank. But like Peter and John, you will dig down deep and find a strength you didn't have. It will not just be emotion or adrenaline but the grace and power that come from almighty God. Exhausted yet pursuing.

You are a person who has been put on this earth for such a time as this, so you can be tired and still do amazing things. Do not believe the lie that you have to have everything in order or have a full tank to accomplish the plans and purposes God has for you. You can be sad, you can be tired, you can be weighed down, and you can still keep up the pursuit.

Now, some of you really need to hear this. Others may need to pause, because you've not rested for quite some time and need to recharge your battery so you don't end up burned out on the side of the road. Sabbath is key. Unplugging from busyness and the hustle and bustle of life is essential. Your soul needs to be recharged. And if you have yet to discover how you can come to new life by practicing rhythms of Sabbath, I encourage you to grab some books and learn that principle—that commandment—because it would benefit both you and those you have been called to lead and encourage. Please learn how to rest. I am not a proponent of busyness for busyness's sake. We tell our staff all the time—you don't get extra credit in this environment for burnout, so please make sure you are practicing rhythms of grace and rest so that you can go the long haul.

At the same time, in our day and age of comfort and ease, we are so averse to resistance and difficulty that at the first sign of problems or pain, we think God must not be in it. We think we must be going in the wrong direction, that we somehow missed what we're supposed to do. And that may be true sometimes, but it's not true all the time. Sometimes it's the resistance and the difficulty that show you what you have on the inside. Because if you did not have the pain, you would not understand the depth of the promise that God has for your life. I've heard some say that David needed Goliath, that without Goliath, David would not have known what was on the inside of him. And you need some Goliaths in your life. God in His grace will put you and me in situations that are bigger than us, and He asks us, "Do you trust Me?"

Our church family has been growing spiritually, emotionally, mentally, and numerically. We found ourselves in need of a new building. We were packing people in as much as we possibly could, adding service after service, experience after experience. We knew we just needed a larger space so we could have enough seating for the season God was taking us into. So one day I was praying, and I felt this nudge in the right side of my rib cage, and the still, small voice of the Holy Spirit said, "Earl, go drive around that building at Walnut Hill." I grabbed one of our campus pastors, and Ben and I took off. The second I drove onto the campus, I felt like God said, "This is the next home for Shoreline City Church."

Now, His message was clear to me. But I also saw the building, and it was massive—150,000 square feet sitting on almost eighteen acres, right there off the highway in Dallas, Texas. And as the two of us drove around that building, I knew God was saying this was our next home, but I also felt like I was looking at Goliath. How could we possibly buy this building?

I prayed on it, went back and talked to my wife, and through some beautiful relationships, I found myself sitting face-to-face with the pastor of that church. Highland Oaks Church of Christ was led by a man and a team filled with integrity and love. I sat across from him at Panera Bread in a suburb of Dallas, trying to figure out how I was going to tell a peer of mine and a new friend that God had told me the building he and his church were currently occupying was supposed to be our next home and the headquarters for all our locations. I got up and went to the bathroom and looked at myself in the mirror and thought, *How would you want someone to treat you? That's how you gotta treat him.* So I went back and I was just honest. With as much humility and kindness and respect as I could, I said, "Have you guys ever thought about selling your property? Because we are growing as a church and are wondering about another home. Is your current space right for you, or have you been praying through finding another location?"

Fast-forward, we took a tour of that very building, and I brought some of our lead staff along. Even some of our Guatemala team was present. The tour lasted a couple of hours—that's how large this building was. It felt right. It was right. And it also felt like a mountain. We started the negotiations with humility, respect, and kindness, and it was beautiful to see how God brought everything together. We agreed to purchase the building, and God began to work miracles.

Then I felt God asking me to ask Him for something that seemed incredibly impossible.

"Earl, I want you to trust Me. I want you to ask Me to move you into this building debt-free." Gulp. Debt-free? Now, we had done our due diligence. We had talked with our board, got with our financial institutions, dotted our *i*'s, and crossed our *t*'s. We were sure we had taken care of the logistical and administrative details and had made wise choices. We wanted to have everything in order. But we still knew that God was asking us to do something that was bigger than we were able to do in our own strength. Yeah, we could buy the building and make payments, but God was asking us for something even more significant—not only to believe Him for this building but to believe Him for this building debt-free. So we started the journey. We saw people step up and say, "I wanna be a part of this beautiful mission to make it on earth as it is in heaven." As of the writing of this book, we are not debt-free at all, but we are still believing God. We're moving forward, and money is coming in, but we are still asking God for the impossible, and my faith is being stretched.

But let me tell you, God had the audacity to go ahead and stretch me even more.

We have a campus in North Dallas, and that campus was a mobile location for years until a building became available in Frisco. This building was about ten thousand square feet, would seat a few hundred people, and would allow this campus to have a consistent space to gather. This new location would enable the north campus to serve the surrounding community with an even greater level of effectiveness and strength. And that's when I heard God say, "You should buy this building too."

Wait, what? Two buildings at the same time. I was thinking, *God, are You really going to take me out of my comfort zone this much?* So again, we went back to prayer and then back to our board. Again, we talked with our financial experts and said, "Okay, we're going to take this step of faith too. We just want you to know that God is asking us to do some things that we cannot do ourselves."

Understand that gathering wisdom and good counsel

and submitting to authority are all essential as you navigate taking steps of faith. But God is not averse to putting us in situations where we cannot succeed except by His hand of power and grace. So if you are looking at your vision and purpose and you can accomplish it by yourself, then I submit that you may be dreaming too small and there's probably more to come.

So here we are at Shoreline Church, believing God for miracles. And even though we're believing Him for miracles—and believe He has prepared the way—we still have to keep on pursuing. We still have to get demo teams in the buildings and rip up carpets and remove old bookcases and rally the troops. We're still casting vision and having meetings and praying audacious prayers. We still have a part to play. We know God's part is the most important, but that doesn't mean we don't have a role to play. As we partner with the Creator of all things, we are reminding our souls that since this is His church and His vision and these are His people, He will be the one to accomplish what He has set before us. Because at the end of the day, this is all about Him and His glory.

> You weren't called to safety. You were called to surrender and to adventure.

Whether it's a church, a for-profit business, or a family— whatever it is—God is at the center, and He will empower you to accomplish the plan and purpose He has for you. Rest assured, there will be times you will feel intimidated, exhausted, maybe even fearful, but do not stop pursuing. You weren't called to safety. You were called to surrender and to adventure.

Look at the switch that happens in Gideon.

> Gideon and his three hundred men, exhausted yet keeping up the pursuit, came to the Jordan and crossed it. He said to the men of Sukkoth, "Give my troops some bread; they are worn out, and I am still pursuing Zebah and Zalmunna, the kings of Midian."
>
> But the officials of Sukkoth said, "Do you already have the hands of Zebah and Zalmunna in your possession? Why should we give bread to your troops?"
>
> Then Gideon replied, "Just for that, when the LORD has given Zebah and Zalmunna into my hand, I will tear your flesh with desert thorns and briers." (Judges 8:4–7)

Do you see the fire in this man? Do you see the switch that has happened? He went from "I'm not sure" to "I'm about to tear flesh with desert thorns and briers." Gideon has gone from hiding to now standing up boldly. Do you see that he has switched from being a man who continued to doubt himself to being a man who put his confidence in God and what God had called him to do? I want this same switch to happen in every single one of us. If you are reading this, I'm declaring over your life that this will be a prophetic shift for you.

You will not think the same.

You will not pray the same.

You will not stand the same.

You will not walk the same.

You will step further and more fully into who God has called you to be.

And you will stand with confidence, knowing that your confidence is found in the finished work of Jesus Christ. And there will be people who will doubt what you're doing, and they'll question what God has put in your hands, but you go ahead and speak with confidence, because God is on your side and He is going before you to prepare the way.

You're part of His church. It's time to get off the ropes and stop taking all these hits. It's time to go on the offensive. It's time to attack.

For the record, I don't mean it's time for you to do whatever you wanna do, whenever you wanna do it, whatever makes you feel good. Be very, very careful of how our flesh and our sneaky pride can distort a pure purpose and intention. Please be mindful of that. But I do not want you to be so mindful of the pitfalls that you don't move forward in your purpose. This has been my struggle for far too long. I don't want to be seen as prideful. I don't want to get ahead of God. I don't want to somehow stain the name and the work of Jesus. But in keeping my eyes on me instead of God, I've sought safety instead of moving forward with the determination with which Christ has called me to live. So, yes, there are pitfalls.

Pride is real.

Ego is real.

Selfishness is real.

Greed is real.

I don't think we can turn a blind eye to any of those things, but Gideon's act of bowing down and worshipping can inform how we stand up and lead. As I keep my eyes fixed on Jesus and not on my influence or popularity, I intentionally ask God to keep me on my knees.

I've already shared with you my favorite scripture, and it serves us well to reflect on it again: "[Jesus] must become greater; I must become less."[9] Those are the words that I want branded and tattooed on my heart. And I want the "words of my mouth and this meditation of my heart [to] be pleasing in [His] sight."[10] I want to clothe myself in humility and love—or rather, I've already been clothed in those things by what Jesus Christ did for me on the cross, and now I want to walk in them completely and fully.

Jesus is the picture of humility. Yes, He washed feet.[11] Yes, He became "obedient to death—even death on a cross!"[12] And He also had a fire in His belly whereby He understood He was not representing Himself, but He was on assignment from God.[13] I wanna wake up your prophetic assignment. I strongly encourage you to seek the face of God and the heart of God so clearly and so passionately that you can't help but move forward to who God has called you to be as you serve His purposes in your generation.

It's your time to say yes to the switch.

10
FINISH WELL

My wife and I took a trip out of town to celebrate our anniversary, and while away, we decided to watch a movie. We love watching movies together. To be more specific, my wife loves the movie to be on while she falls asleep on my shoulder, and I end up watching it by myself. But we heard the movie *Elvis* that came out in 2022 was pretty remarkable, so we decided to watch it, and it was fascinating. The cinematography, the colors, and the story were compelling. I didn't know much about Elvis Presley, but I knew the guy started impressively but didn't have the type of ending that any of us would have wanted.

He was honestly one of the most popular artists of the twentieth century—incredibly gifted. He appeared on *The Ed Sullivan Show* for the first time in 1956.[1] And his career was filled with hit record after hit record after hit record. The movie touched on the fact that in the days when Elvis was getting his start, the chasm between Black people and White people in America seemed insurmountable. Music that Black people in America enjoyed and played could not be purchased as easily, and there was no crossover from a Black artist to the White community. When Elvis came on the scene, he had an ability to play blues music with tremendous passion and zeal, and he was able to introduce it to a White audience because he himself was White, and his popularity skyrocketed.[2] This man was known all over the world. If Instagram had been around back then, he would've had at least half a billion followers. But even with all his popularity and fame and talent, he didn't end well.

His life slowly began to deteriorate with a mix of prescription drugs and alcohol. I assume the pressures of life and the brokenness that we all have in us began to eat away at the man's soul. He had suffered a couple of overdoses, even one that put him in a coma. He had become overweight. His health was deteriorating, and he slurred his words. Then on August 16, 1977, he was found dead on the floor of his bathroom.[3] His life didn't end the way he or anyone would have wanted. And so we see the same with Gideon.

"No sooner had Gideon died than the Israelites again prostituted themselves to the Baals."[4] We might guess at first glance that since things didn't plummet until after Gideon died, he had nothing to do with the downturn. How could he? He was dead! He was no longer around to correct them or give them the leadership and direction they needed.

Judges 8:28 tells us, "Midian was subdued before the Israelites and did not raise its head again. During Gideon's lifetime, the land had peace forty years." After God used Gideon in a mighty, powerful way, there was a generation of peace. But once Gideon died, the people turned their backs on God right away. So the question is, Why would they turn so quickly? There may be some hints in the text.

> The Israelites said to Gideon, "Rule over us— you, your son and your grandson—because you have saved us from the hand of Midian."
>
> But Gideon told them, "I will not rule over you, nor will my son rule over you. The LORD will rule over you." And he said, "I do have one request, that each of you give me an earring from your share of the plunder." (It was the custom of the Ishmaelites to wear gold earrings.)
>
> They answered, "We'll be glad to give them." So they spread out a garment, and each of them threw a ring from his plunder onto it. The weight of the gold rings he asked for came to seventeen hundred shekels, not counting the ornaments, the pendants and the purple garments worn by the kings of Midian or the chains that were on their camels' necks. Gideon made the gold into an ephod, which he placed in Ophrah, his town. All Israel prostituted themselves by worshiping it there, and it became a snare to Gideon and his family. (Judges 8:22–27)

Gideon initially pushed back the praise of the people, which seems incredibly noble. Then he asked for gold, which makes some sense after he led the people in such a victorious battle. But then he turned the gold into an ephod. This ephod was a linen shirtlike garment worn by the priests of Israel. Gideon made it and fashioned it with the gold. Then the people began to prostitute themselves by worshipping it.

Now, some would argue that Gideon did not make this ephod so people would worship it. Perhaps he made it as a reminder for the people of what God had done to bring them out of bondage and captivity. Even if we give Gideon the benefit of the doubt, what we know for sure from Scripture is that "Israel prostituted themselves by worshiping it there, and it became a snare to Gideon and his family."

So while Gideon was living, he saw the snare that his creation had become. He saw all of Israel prostituting themselves in front of it. And after he died, Israel continued down that road and ended up worshipping false gods.

I'm sure this ending was not the one Gideon would have wanted. And I'm convinced it didn't end the way God wanted it to, either, because God didn't want His children—His chosen people—returning to prostituting themselves. Here they were, stepping into the same cycle. Here they were, getting back on that terrible amusement ride—the Gravitron. Here they were, about to spin and spin and spin and be stuck in a cycle of idolatry and bondage.

God had raised up a leader to take them out of that place of bondage. But toward the end of his life and after he passed from this life into the next, the people he had been called to lead prostituted themselves.

I've heard it said that life's not about how you start; it's about how you finish. And I think that's true. You can start from way behind, but if you continue the pursuit, you can make up some significant ground, and people will remember the end rather than the beginning. But even with that being the case, I would love to start well and end well and live well in the middle.

> **Start well and end well and live well in the middle.**

But if you're anything like me, there have been bumps in the road at some point in time. Few of us, if any, have had a straight-line journey. And if it has been a straight line for you, just recognize there is a curveball coming, because Jesus said, "In this world you will have trouble. But take heart! I have overcome the world."[5]

You see, there is a generational effect to our actions. It's important for you and me to understand that God is not interested just in us doing well; He's also interested in us passing the baton to the next generation so they can do well.

Sometimes those of us who are younger don't think about the next generation, because we think it's all about us. But the reality is, every generation who thought it was all about them eventually became the old generation and then passed on to the next life, leaving their legacy for others to endure or stand upon.

When I was about thirteen years old, I was at a summer camp, and we had a relay competition. All of us were at a university track, and we were running the four-by-one-hundred, which means four people would each run one hundred meters. I was kind of fast at the time, so I was given the honor and the responsibility to run the last leg and close whatever gap existed between our team and the competition.

The thing about a relay race is you don't get to run until the baton is in your hands. The gun sounds, and the first runner takes off, baton in hand. The second-leg runner is ready and waiting for that baton. Now the second runner can run a little bit to get up to speed, but they can't cross outside of the transition zone. If they do, they're disqualified.

So runner two took off, then runner three. The third runner rounded the corner. I began to take a few steps, he put the baton in my hand, and I ran as fast as I possibly could. But by then, we were already well behind the other teams. The speed and consistency of my predecessors affected my start.

Now, I'm not throwing any shade on them. We got seventh place and even a ribbon. Though I don't think you should ever get a ribbon for seventh place—let me just make that known. But this baton passing, this relay race, is a picture of life. Someone came before Gideon, and someone was coming after Gideon, and we want to do all we can for those who follow us.

Think about the people in your life whom you really respect. Think about the business leader you want to be like, the man or woman you'd like to emulate, the marriage you want to follow. Think about the person you hope to imitate for your generation. Who do you want to be like as a parent, spouse, leader, or friend?

Who do you want to be like as a student, a president, or a CEO? Who do you want to be like as a supervisor or a manager? Who is it you want to emulate? They are the ones who ran the leg ahead of you, the ones you're watching. You are getting the baton from them.

I look at my grandparents having been married over sixty years, and I want a marriage that lasts through the decades like theirs did. I look at other people who stayed the course, who are pastors and leaders, and who live lives of integrity and humility. They passed on to the next generation what God had given them to do—leaving things in order and strong, not marred by controversy and sin, but draped in the garment of integrity and service and love. I recognize, since I got the baton from them, I can't be so focused on my race that I forget there's a baton in my hand that I'll have to pass on. I am moving forward and so are you. Our purpose doesn't end with us. It continues beyond us because our purpose was birthed in the heart of God and given for us to steward in our generation.

We get a little glimpse about Gideon's son in Scripture. In Judges 8:18, the Midianite leaders, Zebah and Zalmunna, admit to killing Gideon's brothers. Gideon replied, "'As surely as the LORD lives, if you had spared their lives, I would not kill you.' Turning to Jether, his oldest son, he said, 'Kill them!' But Jether did not draw his sword, because he was only a boy and was afraid."[6] This was after Gideon had changed and switched and had gone in pursuit. After he had hunted down these other leaders, after he was now ready to exact justice on their lives, he turned to his oldest son and said, "Son, you go ahead and do it. You handle what needs to be handled right here." But the son did not do it, "because he was only a boy and was afraid." Afraid. How many times did we read in Judges 6–7 that Gideon was afraid? How many times did we read over these few pages that Gideon was being led not by conviction but by fear? How many times did we see Gideon take steps backward? Not because God wasn't calling him, but because he was afraid to move forward. And now look at his oldest son. I don't want to be hard on him, but Gideon's son did not do what his father asked him to do—not because he didn't know how to do it, but because he was afraid to do it. Courage wasn't passed down to the next generation.

Courage wasn't passed down to the next generation.

Each of our wonderful kids has had their moments of being afraid. I remember when Parker, our oldest, was about seven years old and I actually asked him to stomp on one of those crazy Texas flying roaches that grow on trees. I don't know where these terrible insects came from, but they are absolutely deplorable and make it clear that there must be a devil and a hell because these things are treacherous. Well, there was one that had made its way into the back room, and I asked Parker to step on it. He wouldn't do it.

The thing is, it was already dead. I just needed him to get over his fear and crush it. Now, I don't know if he knew that it was dead or not, but I'm telling you, I stayed with him for one hour while he wrestled with stomping his foot on that spawn of Satan. I saw it as a moment when I didn't want fear to hold on to his life. I didn't want fear to be the loudest voice in his head. And if he was going to accomplish what God had called him to accomplish, he would have to be able to confront the fear and move forward.

Why did I know what he was facing? Because I had faced the same thing myself, and I didn't want my son living in the same prison I had lived in. So I got one of my combat boots, put it on his foot, and told him how much bigger he was and how much bigger that boot was. Then I implored and encouraged and challenged and pushed Parker to drop his foot on that despicable roach. And he cried and said he didn't want to, but I wasn't going to let up, because I did not want fear to dictate his future.

"Do it, son. Do it scared."

As his foot hovered above that insect, he shouted over and over, "I can't do it."

And I shouted back, "Yes, you can. You can do it. Yes, you can. You are a warrior. You are strong."

As tears flowed down his cute seven-year-old cheeks, I

continued to tell him, "You've got this, Parker. You can do this. You're stronger than you know." After an hour of encouragement and prodding and challenge—and if I'm honest, I probably made some small threat because my patience grew thin—my son dropped that foot on that roach.

And now I see my son living not a life of fear but a life of faith. I think when he was seven, God was giving us an opportunity to prepare him for when he would be seventeen and twenty-seven and beyond. I had the same moments with my second son, Grayson. He didn't like the dark, and I get it—there are times I don't like the dark either. Shoot, I still remember those walks back from my friend's house on the dark country roads in New Jersey. I know how your mind can mess with you in the dark, but I also know the truth, and I don't want to be timid with that fear.

I also don't want my son in bondage to fear. So when he was twelve, I grabbed him, hugged him, looked him in the eye, and talked to him as a father, a drill sergeant, a coach, and a friend. I turned off all the lights down the hallway and said, "Grayson, go walk. Go touch that door at the end of the hall while the lights are off, and come all the way back." And he didn't want to do it. He didn't want to take the step. But I didn't want his future to be riddled with fear.

Because if God is asking me to overcome fear in my generation, I don't want to pass on that same fear to his generation. It didn't take as long with Grayson—he was a little bit older and a little bit bigger. He took steps down the hallway, touched that door, and came on back.

We had to do the same thing with our precious daughter.

We were at the park one morning, and I was pushing her on the swing. It was early, so no one else was there. She had brought her doll with her, and she asked me to put it in the next swing and to push both of them at the same time. So like any good dad hanging out with his beautiful daughter, I pushed both Elle and her doll back and forth, back and forth, for quite some time. Elle continued to say, "Higher, Daddy, higher. Higher, Daddy, higher." She was speaking about herself, not her doll, because I was corrected rather quickly when I pushed her baby doll too high and she told me, "Daddy, she doesn't like that."

"I'm sorry, Elle. Obviously, you know best." But she asked for me to push her over and over and over again, and so I did.

Then I said, "Hey, Elle, have you ever jumped off the swing? When you're on your way forward, if you release your hands from the swing, the momentum will carry you. You'll fly through the air a little bit and land on your feet, I hope. It's a fantastic experience."

"No, Daddy, no thank you."

"Come on, Elle, let's do it. Just try."

I must be honest: I did not push my daughter as much as I pushed my sons, which was not right. But I quickly came to my senses because I recognized that this little girl is gonna grow up to be a woman in a world that will not always play nice, and I want to prepare her for what is to come. So I mustered up all the kindness and challenge I could and said, "Hey, Elle, I want you to try it. I'll even show you how to do it."

And eventually, after some encouragement, she took the step and jumped off the swing.

I wanna pass a baton of faith to my kids, not a baton of fear. I want to pass a baton of strength, not one of insecurity and doubt.

Now, I know I'm gonna be wrestling with some things for the rest of my life. I think God keeps some things in our lives to remind us of our weaknesses so that Christ's power can rest on us.[7] I do see that, but I'm going to be incredibly diligent, and my wife is by my side as we live our lives for the glory of God and pass on to our kids not a spirit of living safe but a heart of surrender and adventure for the glory and the cause of Jesus Christ. There's a fire that I want to have in our bellies.

I don't know if Gideon was thinking about what it would be like when he passed, but I'm thinking about it. I want to make sure I'm leaving a legacy and instilling virtues inside my kids and my church and my friends—dare I even say, this generation—that we may live our lives not for ourselves but for the fame and glory of Jesus Christ.

We've talked about how words matter. We've talked about how we've made a switch.

One Vision Sunday—a day we at Shoreline City Church set aside to give direction and focus for our church community—I had to share with my church what I call our constitution. God dropped some words in my heart one day as I prayed. I first shared them with the staff, and then I shared them with the church. I had our staff sign what I'd written, and I gave our church copies:

We, the people of Shoreline City, in order to make it on earth as it is in heaven, sign and establish this constitution for our church family. I believe, stand by, and promote the following: God is good. Jesus is alive. The Spirit is working. The Bible is the Word of God. The gospel is true. The cross and the empty grave are our message. Love is our motivation. People are our passion. Development is our joy. The 12 Stones are our boundaries.[8] Discord is a poison. Encouragement is our sound. Faith is our posture. Confrontation is necessary. Unity is our aim. Less of us and more of Him is our prayer. Character is our currency. Excellence is our standard. Forward is our direction. From our knees is where we lead. Prayer is our secret sauce. Worship is our weapon. Kindness is our fragrance. Victory is our anthem. Darkness is defeated. The devil is a liar. Our perspective is 360 degrees. Growth is our expectation. Wisdom is our inheritance. Peace is our guard. Authentic is our spirit. Silos are our enemy. Giving is our honor. Change is our normal. Miracles still happen. Revival is now. Systems and structures are our servant. Hope is our outlook. Honest is our assessment. Soft are our hearts. Thick is our skin. Diverse is our family. Joyful is our attitude. Anointed are our lives. Adopted is our position. Blessed, favored, and called is our team.

That is what I'm passing on to the next generation.

What are you passing on? What is your *why* for who you are and how your life matters?

It's time to say yes to becoming who God is calling you to be. We have said no enough times. We have said no over and over and over again, and we've made excuses like Gideon did, and we've disqualified ourselves so many times. But in this moment and on these last few pages, may our hearts burst with excitement, faith, and anticipation. Let us say, "Here am I, Lord. Use me."[9]

Let us say, "Here am I, Lord. Use me."

Our glorious Savior faced so many battles. He faced so many moments when He could have thrown in the towel. John 12:27–28 gives us a peek into one such moment, when Jesus said,

> "Now my soul is troubled, and what shall I say? 'Father, save me from this hour'? No, it was for this very reason I came to this hour. Father, glorify your name!"
>
> Then a voice came from heaven, "I have glorified it, and will glorify it again."

These verses make it clear what Jesus was feeling. His soul was troubled. There was difficulty ahead. And yet Jesus refused to pray the prayers so many of us make in times of trouble: "God, get me out of this." "God, make the pain go away." "God, make it stop." I understand those prayers, those desperate pleas for help. I have said or prayed similar things. But there are some times when that's not the right prayer to pray. What would our lives look like if we prayed instead, "Yeah, God, if You want to take away the pain, by all means go ahead and remove the pain. But, Father, even if You don't take away the pain . . . I will still trust You and follow You"?

This is the faith we see displayed in those three Hebrew men—Shadrach, Meshach, and Abednego—when they were faced with being thrown into the fiery furnace. They said to King Nebuchadnezzar, "If we are thrown into the blazing furnace, the God we serve is able to deliver us from it, and he will deliver us from Your Majesty's hand. But even if he does not, we want you to know, Your Majesty, that we will not serve your gods or worship the image of gold you have set up."[10]

It's the same spirit of faith in Jesus when He said, "It was for this very reason I came to this hour."[11] And can I tell you it's for this very reason that you came to this hour, and it's for this very reason and this very hour that you were born? You could have been born in any generation. You could have been born at any time, but God saw fit for you to be born in this day and age. He knew the family that you would be born into. He knew the family that would raise you. He knew all the challenges that would come your way. He knew all the gifts that He put on the inside of you, and now He is asking you to say yes to His plan and to His will and to His purpose. It was for this very reason you've come to this hour.

So do not let the discord, racism, sexism, poverty, destruction, fear, lies, and distortions be the things that intimidate you and make you run to some corner. At every turn, may these words rise up from your heart: "Father, glorify Your name."

And may you hear God answering back from heaven and saying over your life, "I have glorified it, and I will glorify it again. I glorified My name in Genesis when I made the heavens and the earth. I glorified My name when I parted the Red Sea for the children of Israel. I glorified it when I, Jesus, defeated death, hell, and the grave. When I spoke to Gideon under the oak and when I led him into battle. From generation to generation, I glorified My name. I'm gonna glorify it again today through you. I'm going to glorify My name through every single person who is willing to stay the course, not throw in the towel, live a life of bowed-down worship and surrender, and say, 'God, not my will, but Your will be done on earth as it is in heaven.'"

You have made it this far—now it's time to take the next step. You are breaking free from the cycle. The Gravitron doesn't have the final say in your life. The voice that's been lying to you doesn't have the final say. Your insecurities are not your identity. You have been made new!

So I speak life over you where others have declared death. I speak hope over you where you have walked in doubt. I speak faith over you where there has been fear. And I pray for you to make the move now instead of allowing

another moment to pass by living smaller than the heavenly
calling you have in Christ Jesus.

> You are free.
> You are loved.
> You are called.
> You are chosen.
> You are forgiven.
> You are adopted.
> You are anointed.

And in Jesus's name, you have your spirit back!

ACKNOWLEDGMENTS

This book is the culmination of so many people who've given life and direction to me over the years.

My wife is my best friend and an absolute rock. I've got nothing to write if she's not by my side. My kids, Parker, Grayson, and Elle, were my primary motivation for writing this. I wanted to break a ceiling over my life to create space for each of you to be all God has called you to be. No matter what, my love for you never changes. I am your biggest fan, and I'm in your corner.

To my mom, who told me from a young age, "Don't let anyone else build your world for you, because if you do, they will build it too small." You are strength personified.

To the Shoreline City staff, serve team, and church, I LOVE YOU. You have helped me grow in ways I never knew were possible.

To Alex, Estee, and all the behind-the-scenes book people, thank you.

To all the friends and family who prayed and stayed the course, your example and encouragement have meant the world. Thank you for not quitting.

NOTES

INTRODUCTION: MORE IN YOU

1. LaToshia Butler and Ebonyque Taylor, "A Second Chance: The Impact of Unsuccessful Reentry and the Need for Reintegration Resources in Communities," The Community Policing Dispatch, Office of Community Oriented Policing Services, April 2022, https://cops.usdoj.gov/html/dispatch/04-2022/reintegration_resources.html.

CHAPTER 1: I DON'T LIKE THIS RIDE

1. Judges 3:7.

2. Romans 3:23.

3. Genesis 25:1–2.

4. Exodus 2:16–21.

5. Exodus 18:14–26.

6. Numbers 25.

7. Numbers 25.

8. Numbers 22:4–6.

9. Numbers 31:5–11.

10. Judges 6:5.

11. Judges 6:6.

12. James 4:6.

CHAPTER 2: UNDER THE OAK

1. Chip Heath and Dan Heath, *The Power of Moments: Why Certain Experiences Have Extraordinary Impact* (New York: Simon & Schuster, 2017), 18–19.

2. Genesis 1:27–28.

3. Deuteronomy 5:21.

4. Philippians 3:14.

5. 1 Samuel 17.

6. Mark 1:5–6.

7. See Luke 3:16.

8. Matthew 6:10.

CHAPTER 3: THE STRENGTH YOU HAVE

1. Judges 6:12.

2. Judges 6:13.

3. Ephesians 3:20.

4. Judges 6:13.

5. Judges 6:14.

6. Psalm 139:13.

7. Judges 6:15.

CHAPTER 4: THE ESSENTIALS YOU NEED

1. John 15:5.

2. Exodus 3:12.

3. See Judges 6:14, 16.

4. Romans 2:4.

CHAPTER 5: DO IT SCARED

1. Judges 6:23.

2. Philippians 4:7.

3. Mark 4:35–41.

4. Colossians 1:17.

5. Colossians 3:15.

CHAPTER 6: A HOLY MISSION

1. John 1:1; Colossians 1:15–17.

2. Luke 3:22.

3. John 14:26.

4. Matthew 3:11.

5. Acts 1:4–5, 8.

6. Acts 2:12.

7. Acts 2:17–21.

8. Matthew 6:10.

CHAPTER 7: NOT ENOUGH IS ALL YOU NEED

1. Judges 6:19–21.

2. Hebrews 11:33–34.

3. Judges 6:37.

4. Proverbs 3:5–6.

5. Ephesians 3:20.

CHAPTER 8: WORDS OF POWER

1. Judges 6:15.

2. Genesis 41:51–52.

3. Genesis 48:13–14.

4. Genesis 48:20.

5. Judges 7:10–12.

6. Judges 7:13–14.

7. Judges 7:15.

8. Galatians 2:20.

CHAPTER 9: THE SWITCH AND THE CHASE

1. Roland Martin, "Rumble in the Jungle," *Encyclopaedia Britannica*, last modified May 3, 2024, www.britannica.com/sports/Rumble-in-the-Jungle.

2. Amanda Onion et al., "Muhammad Ali Wins the Rumble in the Jungle," History.com, last modified October 26, 2021, www.history.com/this-day-in-history/muhammad-ali-wins-the-rumble-in-the-jungle.

3. Judges 7:24.

4. Judges 7:23.

5. 2 Corinthians 10:4.

6. Ray Vander Laan, "Gates of Hell," That the World May Know, accessed April 17, 2024, www.thattheworldmayknow.com/gates-of-hell-article.

7. 2 Corinthians 10:3.

8. Matthew 28:19.

9. John 3:30.

10. Psalm 19:14.

11. John 13:1–17.

12. Philippians 2:8.

13. John 6:38.

CHAPTER 10: FINISH WELL

1. "Artists—Elvis Presley," *The Ed Sullivan Show*, accessed June 27, 2024, www.edsullivan.com/artists/elvis-presley.

2. Jon Meacham, "Elvis in the Heart of America," *Time*, August 10, 2017, https://time.com/4894995/elvis-in-the-heart-of-america.

3. Meacham, "Elvis in the Heart of America."

4. Judges 8:33.

5. John 16:33.

6. Judges 8:19–20.

7. 2 Corinthians 12:9.

8. For those wondering, the 12 Stones refer to the values of Shoreline City Church. They can be found here: www.shorelinecity.church/whoweare.

9. See Isaiah 6:8.

10. Daniel 3:17–18.

11. John 12:27.

ABOUT THE AUTHOR

EARL MCCLELLAN is the founder and lead pastor of Shoreline City Church, a thriving faith community with campuses throughout Texas and Guatemala. Earl, his wife Oneka, and their pastoral team have a mission to make it on earth as it is in heaven. Earl is a frequent speaker at influential events both in the States and overseas. His love for people, humor, vulnerability, and strong leadership have brought hope and strength to people in all walks of life. Earl, Oneka, their three children, and a dog he's still not sure about live in Dallas, Texas.